I0122053

Color On! Anthology

Volume 2: January – March 2016

This book belongs to:

_____

This anthology is dedicated to everyone who helps make *Color On! Magazine* possible.

To Anisa, Shelly, Stephanie and Lexi – you guys do so much I can't even begin to enumerate it all.
You're the core of my support team for this adventure, and I couldn't do it without you.
Thank you from the bottom of my heart!

To all of the artists and authors who submit work to the magazine. Needless to say, without your submissions, we wouldn't have a magazine! The quality of your contributions is always wonderful, and we truly appreciate your willingness to share your creations with us.

To the admins of my Facebook group Coloring Books for Adults. My ever-growing team of volunteer admins help the group function smoothly, allowing over 40,000 colorists (so far!) to share their colored works, help our coloring book artists interact with our members, and generally make it possible for everyone to talk about all things coloring. Without them, the group would never succeed.
Thank you so very, very much!

And to our coloring team, a group of amazing coloring artists! Alex, Anne, Barbara B, Barbara H, Bonny, Carolyn, Deanna, Dwayne, Geri, Jane, Jennifer, John, Juanita, Kaila, Larry, Liz, Melissa C, Melissa G, Melissa P, Renee, Sandy, Shelly D, Shelly P, Stephanie, Susan, Tim, Tracey, and Travis.
You guys constantly amaze me with how beautifully you bring our designs to life.
Giant cookies for all of you!!

ISBN: 069266873X
ISBN-13: 978-0692668733

Introduction

Welcome to *Color On! Anthology, Volume 2*. As with all of our anthologies, the designs are printed on one side of the page, and we use the back of each page to give you a bit of insight into our artists. This includes the *Color On! Magazine* interviews with each of our feature artists, plus bios for our other contributing artists, along with information on where you can find their books or art for sale.

Many of the designs in this anthology are exclusive, first offered only to subscribers of *Color On! Magazine*. Now you too can enjoy these designs!

This anthology contains designs from the January, February and March 2016 issues. There are all sorts of animals - cats, squirrels, cows, bunnies, narwhals, a monkey, a llama, and even a moose on skates! You'll find fantastical dragons, ninjas, mermaids and robots. We have holiday designs for Mardi Gras, Chinese New Year and Easter. Beautiful mandalas and lovely scenery have their spots, too! Our artists have created gorgeous designs - you're sure to find something you'll like!

Color on!

The Color On! Team

Tangitude Publications

Editor-in-Chief
Mary J. Winters-Meyer

Marketing Marshal
Anisa A. Claire

Brainstorming Ninjas
Shelly Durham & Stephanie Anders

Artists

Wendy Piersall

J.A. Early Riser & T.J. Crayons

Arto Törmänen (Vivid Owl Coloring)

Alicia Nees

Anisa A. Claire

Anne Manera

Cesar Valtierra

Dwayne Wright

Gayle Daufel-Barff

Jason Hamilton

Joe Shivery

Julian Trocaru

Karlon Douglas

Komfort Wiafe

Mary J. Winters-Meyer

Olivia Julius Dunggat

Penny Farthing Graphics

Rick St. Dennis

Sena Carroz

Tracey Johnston

Valerie, Harry and the Fisch

Valpyra Skullstyr

Color On! Magazine is a digital magazine founded by Mary J. Winters-Meyer and Shyla Jannusch, published monthly by Tangitude Publications, P.O. Box 17623, Urbana, IL 61803-7623. For subscription information, visit http://ColorOnMag.com.

January 2016 Feature Artist Wendy Piersall

By Mary J. Winters-Meyer

This month we have the pleasure of exploring the creative world of Wendy Piersall. Her journey has been less of a straight highway from childhood crayons to adult art, and more of a twisting, winding, loop-the-loop path from artistic aspiration through online entrepreneurship, eventually leading back to art and coloring books.

Color On!: You've mentioned that a publisher approached you about some mandalas you had previously drawn. What made you start drawing mandalas? Were they similar in style to what you created for your coloring books?

Wendy: I started drawing mandalas for the most uninteresting reason of all time: I'd done keyword research and found out that people were looking for mandala coloring pages, so I drew some for my kid's activities blog at WooJr.com. But unlike the other coloring pages I was creating at the time, I found myself to be very relaxed when I was done drawing mandalas - as if I had been meditating. It was because of that amazing experience that I drew 30-40 of them back in 2009 instead of a standard set of 6 that I normally created. They aren't a very similar style to what I've drawn for my books, because they were a combination of drawing plus clip art I had licensed. Everything in my books I draw myself.

Color On!: You talk about your coloring books bringing you "full circle" in your love of art, which is somewhat interesting considering your journey ended up with you creating mandalas. If you had to describe your journey as a mandala, what would it look like?

Wendy: This is SUCH a cool question!! But it's difficult to answer - my career journey has been a very zig-zaggy, eclectic experience. I went from being an artist, to being a corporate trainer, to being a graphic designer, to being a recruiter, to being a business development executive, to being a blogger, and then BACK to being an artist again through my coloring books. So, if you could imagine a mandala that is both chaotic and yet divinely guided - then that's what my journey as a mandala has looked like. I guess I could sum up both my career and drawing mandalas as an exercise in "trusting the process". Both can start out weird and look like crap at times, but if I trust the process of drawing (as I did with my career moves) it always looks beautiful in the end.

Color On!: You've had a lot of success with online businesses, and the explosion of interest in coloring has led a lot of artists to try to make a success in an online environment. What can you tell us about your experiences as a coloring book artist, and the skills required to build a successful following online?

Wendy: I literally wrote the book on mom blogging (*Mom Blogging for Dummies* in 2011), and a lot of what made me successful as a blogger has helped me tremendously as a book author/artist. My number 1 advice to people starting out with their own coloring books is to build a following on Facebook and Instagram right away, well before their books come out. Having a mailing list and giving out free samples of your work are also hugely important to building a fan base.

I frankly see a lot of coloring books on bestseller lists that are not drawn by the author, and instead are pieced together with clip art. This means that unfortunately for all of us, great talent will not sell your books - but great PR, marketing and distribution will. Talent is sure helpful, don't get me wrong - but on its' own, talent is not likely to make you or break you. I spend just as much time marketing as I do drawing, and unless you're willing to work twice as hard to promote your work as you do to create the work, getting into the coloring book business isn't a great idea.

Color On!: How do you create your art? Tell us about your process for creating new work.

Wendy: At the beginning when I am brainstorming ideas, I use just a regular #2 pencil and paper. For the book illustrations, I work in Adobe Illustrator with a Wacom drawing tablet. I use the custom symbols and custom brush tools extensively when creating replicating patterns for my mandalas. And now that I'm in the midst of working on my 6th coloring book, I also have many templates set up so that I can just jump right in and have a finished drawing rather quickly.

Color On!: When coloring your own art, what is your favorite medium(s)?

Wendy: My two top favorites are Polychromos pencils and Copic Markers. I prefer the pencils, actually, because I really enjoy layering colors and shading. But since I have carpal tunnel, I can't use them too much or my hands pretty much stop working for a few days. I also like using watercolors, but they aren't very practical most of the time, especially for use in books with regular paper.

Color On!: Do you enjoy relaxing with coloring books by other artists? If so, do you have a favorite artist or book?

Wendy: I do! It's hard not to love Johanna Basford's work, and I'm also a big fan of Millie Marotta, Jenean Morrison and Hanna Karlzon. Their work is gorgeous!

[Continued on Page 4]

Color On!: What color or colors do you most love to work with?

Wendy: In every other area of my life (wardrobe, home décor, collecting other's art, etc.) I prefer a muted palette with limited colors. But when I color in coloring books, I absolutely cannot resist using nearly every single color in the box. And the brighter the colors, the better!

Color On!: Tell us a little bit about your art. Do you have a favorite piece that you created? Do you create other art besides designs for coloring books?

Wendy: Let me preface this answer by saying that I spent the first 44+ years of my life telling myself I couldn't draw. So I adapted my "art" during this time to my horrible limiting belief and I did everything except draw - crafts, graphic design, photography, etc. It wasn't until 2013 when Ulysses Press asked me to do my first coloring book that I actually DREW and found that I wasn't nearly as bad at it as I had been telling myself. So even though I've had a long and pretty successful career, I've only had a career as an actual artist for just over two years.

I could honestly create coloring books for the rest of my life and be 1000% happy with my career. Realistically, though, I don't know if this adult coloring trend will last that long, so I am building up a backup plan. :) I illustrated a gardening book last fall, and I am giving myself drawing lessons in 2016 to be able to draw people and characters better so that I can get work illustrating children's books, greeting cards, and other non-coloring projects.

My favorite book I've done is *Coloring Dream Mandalas*, though I think that my upcoming *Coloring Bird Mandalas* book will be my new favorite. My favorite mandala that I've ever drawn is the woman with the peacock feather hat in Dreams - I even had it tattooed on my back last summer!

Color On!: Other than creating coloring book art, what interesting hobbies or activities do you enjoy?

Wendy: I love going antiquing, and I collect antique books, vintage figurines, Halloween & Christmas decorations and nautical items. I also garden, sew, write, meditate, cook, and I'm an amateur photographer. Most of all I love family time, and I carve out time to spend with my husband and kids at least once a week - more often in the summer.

Color On!: Have you had any memorable responses to your art work from collectors?

Wendy: The most memorable responses I've gotten from people have definitely been the ones who have used coloring my books as a part of their therapy for depression, anxiety or PTSD. While I love to hear compliments on my work, knowing that my art is helping others find their way to happiness is by far the most rewarding thing I've ever done.

Color On!: If you had to choose one superpower, what would it be?

Wendy: I would definitely be a time traveler!! I'm so inspired by vintage art, I would absolutely LOVE to go back in time to the late 1800's and early 1900's and be a part of the art scene back then!

Color On!: Who is your favorite artist or artists?

Wendy: This is a perfect question to follow the last one - I'd say that I'm most inspired and influenced by Gustav Klimt and Alphonse Mucha from the art nouveau period. I also go crazy for the vintage fashion magazine cover illustrations from publications like Vogue, Harper's Bazar and Vanity Fair before photography took over in the 30's/40's. I was also moved to tears once by studying a Van Gogh painting at the Chicago Art Institute - I felt like I was walking around inside the mind of another artist and it was profoundly moving.

Color On!: Is there some person, place or thing that inspires you when you are creating your art?

Wendy: I get most of my art ideas from two places - my morning meditations and my vintage book, magazine and ephemera collection. When I need to drum up inspiration, I meditate, go through my collection, and turn on my favorite playlist that I only listen to while working. The combination of those three pretty much never fail me, even though it works better some days than others!

[Continued on Page 6]

Color On!: Tell us about your plans for 2016. You've created some beautiful non-mandala designs for our magazine, and mentioned you want to do more of that. Are there other books being planned?

Wendy: Yes! My fifth book, *Coloring Flower Mandala Postcards*, is all done and going to press soon, and will be out in the spring of 2016. As mentioned earlier, I am currently working on *Coloring Bird Mandalas* to be coming out in the middle of 2016. I am also planning on self-publishing some non-mandala adult coloring books, because my publisher Ulysses Press and I are talking about working on some new projects that aren't coloring related. That could keep me busy all year, but I'm also taking a few art classes to build up my portfolio to go after other illustration projects such as children's books, greeting cards, and hopefully a line of fabrics. Since I'm such an art career late bloomer, I'm purposefully trying to bite off more than I can chew - I've got no time to let grass grow under my feet! :)

You can learn more about Wendy's work online.
- Full interview online: http://coloronmag.com/article/a-chat-with-wendy-piersall/
- Wendy's website: http://WendyPiersall.com
- Wendy's books on Amazon: http://tinyurl.com/wendysbooks

You can learn more about Wendy's work online.

- Full interview online: http://coloronmag.com/article/a-chat-with-wendy-piersall/
- Wendy's website: http://WendyPiersall.com
- Wendy's books on Amazon: http://tinyurl.com/wendysbooks

You can learn more about Wendy's work online.

- Full interview online: http://coloronmag.com/article/a-chat-with-wendy-piersall/
- Wendy's website: http://WendyPiersall.com
- Wendy's books on Amazon: http://tinyurl.com/wendysbooks

February 2016 Feature Artist J.A. Early Riser & T.J. Crayons

By Mary J. Winters-Meyer

This month we explore the humorous worlds of Canadian writers and artists, Anisa (J.A. Early Riser) and Travis (T.J. Crayons.) J.A.'s unique brand of humor is brought to life in their *Maniacal Confessions* series of books, with feral faeries, sock monsters, warrior gnomes, drama llamas, sugar frenzies, Grumplestiltskins, and other characters that encourage colorists to use their craziest color combinations when coloring them. In this interview, they give us a peek into how they create their wacky coloring books!

Color On!: You have several writing-related online magazines. What made you add coloring books? Is there a connection?

J.A. Early Riser: There is a connection, actually. I'd been writing journal entries as J.A. Early Riser for a few years and always wanted to do something with them, but could never figure out exactly what. Travis (T.J. Crayons) and I discussed making a zombie survival guide, or an illustrated comic-type book, but the ideas never seemed quite right. Then, one day, my friend Juanita, who is mainly responsible for talking us into doing coloring books, came to town and asked if we could check Chapters for adult coloring books. I told her, good luck… that I'd been searching for such a beast my entire life and had never found any. Of course, I had no idea it was trending at the time.

I joined a few coloring groups, actually the very first one I joined was Adult Coloring Group. I was totally inspired by everything I saw and then it hit me… why not do an activity coloring book and use my J.A. Early Riser alter ego. So that's what we did. The first book, *Maniacal Confessions*, was released at the end of July, 2015.

T.J. Crayons: My response to Anisa when she first approached me about doing coloring books together was… "Seriously?? Coloring books?? For adults?! Hahaha!" At the time, I didn't really know that was a thing. But then I thought back to how many times when I wanted to color, I had to buy books with pictures of big trains with happy faces on them and giant bounding cartoon dinosaurs. That sort of killed my drive for coloring. So the thought of making something that I would want to color was very appealing. We were lucky enough to get in when the adult coloring craze was still sort of in its infancy. I'm glad we did because it has grown into quite a massive following now.

Color On!: Most of your books have two versions – a JUST coloring book, and a combined coloring and activity book. Tell us about them. Why did you choose to release them like that?

J.A. Early Riser: We did a lot of market research before we released. There were a few things we noticed… First of all, there were a lot of complaints about the cover picture not being in the book, so we made sure to include our cover. The next thing we noticed was a decent sized demand for single sided pages. People who use pencil crayons don't mind the double sided books, but people who color mainly with markers can't use the double sided books. That's when we decided to release a Just Coloring version on top of the Activity version. The activity version really explains all of the characters and their stories and there are different activities plus bonus coloring sheets in it.

Another reason we released the Just Coloring version is because of the price difference. We wanted to offer a more affordable version of the book. Because the activity books have pages printed in color, and it's much longer than the Just Coloring version, Amazon forces us to list them at a minimum of $16.85 USD.

Color On!: What can you tell us about your experiences being a coloring book artist and the skills required to build a successful following online?

J.A. Early Riser: Hmmm. Not sure about the skills part, to be honest. We just sort of… jumped in and went with it. We spend a lot of time interacting with people in the coloring groups and take the time to comment on their pictures, especially if it's one of our pictures that they've posted. We both enjoy just being in the communities and hanging out with everyone who colors. It's a lot of fun.

The experience has been incredible. Drawing is actually a secondary thing for me. I mainly write, which is another reason I wanted to do the activity books – so I could combine both. Travis mainly draws, but he also writes poetry, so we're a great team for this kind of thing. We're both really enjoying ourselves so far.

[Continued on Page 14]

Design title: *The Ninjas of Time*

Color On!: How do you create your art? Do you create digitally or with pen and pencil? Tell us about your process for creating new work.

T.J. Crayons: I draw digitally, using an art app on my iPad. I spent a lot of time drawing as a teenager and then stopped for a long time. Recently, I picked it up when Anisa decided to open *Writer's Carnival*. She asked me to do all the art on the site and I thought, sure, why not… Haha. I've learned a lot since then.

Anisa typically draws with pencil and paper and then traces it digitally so that our pictures are in the same format. We didn't do that for the first book but have for the rest of them.

I struggled a little bit at first with the humor aspect of it, I've never been great with cartoon characters or coming up with crazy ideas. My focus was more on the patterns, covers and structures. Anisa would mainly brainstorm the nutty characters and scenarios. Eventually, though, I became a part of that process more and have been dipping into drawing my own Absur'D characters, as well.

Color On!: When coloring your own art, what is your favorite medium(s)?

T.J. Crayons: I definitely prefer pencil crayons. I've tried markers and gel pens, they're fun, but I can't shade very well with them.

J.A. Early Riser: I love EVERYTHING! Hah! Pencil crayons, gel pens, markers, pastels… anything I can get my hands on, I use… even highlighters!

Color On!: Do you enjoy relaxing with coloring books by other artists? If so, do you have a favorite artist or book?

J.A. Early Riser: Oh yeah, definitely. Hmmm… I have a few favorites! Well, yours, for starters, Mary! [Editor's note: *Dragons, Knots, Bots and More!*] I also love *Coloring on the Edge* (Karlon Douglas), *Narwhalidays* (Tracey Johnston), Chroma Tomes (especially their Gnome ones), *Color with Komfort: Mind's Eye of a Gypsy*, and then some of the bigger ones would be *Doodle Invasion, Unicorns are Jerks*, the Game of Thrones book. I'm a huge fan of Rick St. Dennis – I absolutely love his work – and From the Broken Mind of Joe's Ink. I could go on and on, but that's a few of them. Oh, and I really like a lot of the artists that have been published in Color On! Magazine, to be 100% honest. I really enjoyed the November issue with Ellen Million.

Color On!: What color or colors do you most love to work with?

T.J. Crayons: Greens and blues and yellows to reds.

J.A. Early Riser: I'm really not a fan of red… I know, I know. But it's true. I rarely use it. I love purples and turquoises. Most recently, I've been enjoying oranges and yellows.

Color On!: Tell us a little bit about your art. Do you have a favorite piece that you created? Do you create other art besides designs for coloring books?

T.J. Crayons: Oh. Tough question. My favorite so far is probably the Frenzy Fabricator in our newest book, *Candy Coated Kaos*. I love the little character's that are hidden in Anisa's head that she brings to life on her pages. They seem to come in extra handy for our latest book, *Candy Coated Kaos*. I was a big fan of the Feral Fairy Hoarder in *Maniacal Confessions* and Angry Chicken Mob in the same book. I do the covers for *Reader's Carnival* and *Long Story Short* magazines and all the site art on *Writer's Carnival, Long Story Short* and *Maniacal Confessions*. I also design book covers for people.

J.A. Early Riser: Not sure I can pick a favorite! I know my favorites so far from Travis are Grumpy Flowers in *Maniacal Confessions*, the Octopus Ride in *Carnival Carnage*, the Ice Cream Globe in *Candy Coated Kaos* and Grumplestiltskin in *Feral Fairy Tales*. For my own picture… I think it's Granny and the Big Sad Wolf in *Feral Fairy Tales*. Other than Absur'D, no, I don't really do much else for art. I'm more of a writer. Well, unless planning parties for people and hand making all the decorations counts. Haha.

[Continued on Page 16]

Design title: *Grumpy Goes to the Beach*

Color On!: Other than creating coloring book art, what interesting hobbies or activities do you enjoy?

J.A. Early Riser: Reading, reading and more reading. Did I mention reading? Haha. Writing stories, playing guitar, playing video games, camping, coloring, weird arts and crafts, animals (is that a hobby? Because I have a lot of them!), gardening, baking sometimes.

T.J. Crayons: Woodworking, writing poetry, camping, playing guitar, coloring, building the perfect campfire, playing video games, drawing.

Color On!: Have you had any memorable responses to your art work from collectors?

T.J. Crayons: Yes. We've had some great responses from the pictures we do from the coloring books. Honestly didn't imagine this would go any further than a little hobby project, but so far the response has been pretty amazing.

J.A. Early Riser: Too many to list! It's been a surreal experience. I was really nervous when we put the first book out, thinking nobody would be interested, but I couldn't be happier with the response so far. It's been incredible.

Color On!: If you had to choose one superpower, what would it be?

T.J. Crayons: Oh, that's easy. Flying. No question. Ever since I was a kid, that's all I've wanted to do.

J.A. Early Riser: I'd definitely want to be able to time travel or something. That would be pretty awesome.

Color On!: Who is your favorite artist or artists?

T.J. Crayons: That's an impossible answer. I really like Karlon Douglas and Rick St. Dennis.

J.A. Early Riser: I already answered above, but if we're talking just art in general… Brian Froud, for sure.

Color On!: Is there some person, place or thing that inspires you when you are creating your art?

T.J. Crayons: Probably not really any one thing. As far as influences go, though, I'm a big fan of Dr. Seuss and always have been. I love the wacky pictures, but more importantly love the way he writes.

J.A. Early Riser: Hmmm. Not really. I live, eat and breathe humor. Love it. Anything that makes me laugh, or others laugh, that's my go to. So I'm constantly thinking about the weirdest things I can possibly think of and that's where I draw my inspiration from.

Color On!: Tell us about your plans for 2016. Are there other books being planned?

T.J. Crayons: Oh, most definitely. I think each book gets a little better than the last and Anisa and I have some more ideas in our head that we'd love to put to paper.

J.A. Early Riser: Way to not spill the beans, hey, Travis? Haha! We're thinking about doing another book in the Faerie Trimmings line, possibly Wizard Wares. Then we'd like to do Baby Absur'Dians and a holiday edition of Absur'D featuring Christmas, Easter, Valentine's Day, New Years and Halloween.

You can learn more about J.A. Early Riser & T.J. Crayons online.
- Full interview online: http://coloronmag.com/article/a-chat-with-absurdians-j-a-early-riser-and-t-j-crayons/
- Their website: http://maniacalconfessions.com
- Their Etsy shop: https://www.etsy.com/shop/ManiacalConfessions
- Join the Weirdos Facebook group: https://www.facebook.com/groups/ColoUringForWeirdos

Design title: *Moose on Skates*

You can learn more about J.A. Early Riser & T.J. Crayons online.

- Full interview online: http://coloronmag.com/article/a-chat-with-absurdians-j-a-early-riser-and-t-j-crayons/
- Their website: http://maniacalconfessions.com
- Their Etsy shop: https://www.etsy.com/shop/ManiacalConfessions
- Join the Weirdos Facebook group: https://www.facebook.com/groups/ColoUringForWeirdos

Design title: *Frenzied*

You can learn more about J.A. Early Riser & T.J. Crayons online.
- Full interview online: http://coloronmag.com/article/a-chat-with-absurdians-j-a-early-riser-and-t-j-crayons/
- Their website: http://maniacalconfessions.com
- Their Etsy shop: https://www.etsy.com/shop/ManiacalConfessions
- Join the Weirdos Facebook group: https://www.facebook.com/groups/ColoUringForWeirdos

TROLL TOOTS

Fairy DUST

Design title: *Troll Toots*
from the Upcoming Baby Absur'Dians Coloring Book

You can learn more about J.A. Early Riser & T.J. Crayons online.

- Full interview online: http://coloronmag.com/article/a-chat-with-absurdians-j-a-early-riser-and-t-j-crayons/
- Their website: http://maniacalconfessions.com
- Their Etsy shop: https://www.etsy.com/shop/ManiacalConfessions
- Join the Weirdos Facebook group: https://www.facebook.com/groups/ColoUringForWeirdos

Design title: *The Gumball Monster*

You can learn more about J.A. Early Riser & T.J. Crayons online.
- Full interview online: http://coloronmag.com/article/a-chat-with-absurdians-j-a-early-riser-and-t-j-crayons/
- Their website: http://maniacalconfessions.com
- Their Etsy shop: https://www.etsy.com/shop/ManiacalConfessions
- Join the Weirdos Facebook group: https://www.facebook.com/groups/ColoUringForWeirdos

Design title: *Snuggle Dumpling*

You can learn more about J.A. Early Riser & T.J. Crayons online.
- Full interview online: http://coloronmag.com/article/a-chat-with-absurdians-j-a-early-riser-and-t-j-crayons/
- Their website: http://maniacalconfessions.com
- Their Etsy shop: https://www.etsy.com/shop/ManiacalConfessions
- Join the Weirdos Facebook group: https://www.facebook.com/groups/ColoUringForWeirdos

FO9 SALE

Design title: *Hey Diddle Diddle & a Twisted Little Fiddle*

You can learn more about J.A. Early Riser & T.J. Crayons online.

- Full interview online: http://coloronmag.com/article/a-chat-with-absurdians-j-a-early-riser-and-t-j-crayons/
- Their website: http://maniacalconfessions.com
- Their Etsy shop: https://www.etsy.com/shop/ManiacalConfessions
- Join the Weirdos Facebook group: https://www.facebook.com/groups/ColoUringForWeirdos

Design title: *Octopus Ride*

You can learn more about J.A. Early Riser & T.J. Crayons online.

- Full interview online: http://coloronmag.com/article/a-chat-with-absurdians-j-a-early-riser-and-t-j-crayons/
- Their website: http://maniacalconfessions.com
- Their Etsy shop: https://www.etsy.com/shop/ManiacalConfessions
- Join the Weirdos Facebook group: https://www.facebook.com/groups/ColoUringForWeirdos

Here comes the ...

Drama
Llama

Design title: *Drama Llama*

You can learn more about J.A. Early Riser & T.J. Crayons online.
- Full interview online: http://coloronmag.com/article/a-chat-with-absurdians-j-a-early-riser-and-t-j-crayons/
- Their website: http://maniacalconfessions.com
- Their Etsy shop: https://www.etsy.com/shop/ManiacalConfessions
- Join the Weirdos Facebook group: https://www.facebook.com/groups/ColoUringForWeirdos

March 2016 Feature Artist Vivid Owl Coloring

with artist Arto Törmänen and manager Mika Haikonen

By Mary J. Winters-Meyer

This month's feature artist, Vivid Owl Coloring, is the brain child of two Finland residents, Arto Törmänen & Mika Haikonen. Arto is the artist who brings us the designs to color, and Mika is the manager who helps Arto create the books and market them. They both were happy to answer questions for *Color On! Magazine* this month.

Color On!: Arto, you're an award-winning graphic designer. Why did you decide to add coloring book artist to your other achievements?

Arto: I draw a lot in my free time, especially with markers. I just start to draw something that comes to my mind and often those drawings turn into fully finished art pieces. When Mika proposed a joint project, I immediately responded "Absolutely, let's do it." I thought that my style of marker drawing would be a good fit for this kind of work.

Color On!: Mika, what made you decide to partner with Arto to start Vivid Owl Coloring? It's very different from your other business ventures.

Mika: In the spring of last year I was feeling that I need to try something new. I had plans for a few things, but I must say launching an adult coloring brand was not one of them! However, I was driving across the country with my girlfriend last summer, and when we stopped at various places I browsed through quite a number of adult coloring books, and thought of an idea I absolutely wanted to try. I then quickly contacted Arto with a project proposal, and I'm so glad he was ready to work on this. We've worked together previously on other projects. I like his drawing and art style a lot and thought it would be excellent style to apply to adult coloring designs. While creating our first book, we founded a company and started to build our business models. Eight weeks after our decision to create an adult coloring book, the first version was ready.

As for the other plans I had, lecturing at a Finnish university was one of the dreams I was able to accomplish. The rest are on the back burner waiting for their time.

Color On!: Your first book is a series of beautiful, artistic designs, with a very sensual undertone. In contrast, your designs in this issue have a very whimsical feel. For example, several of us on my coloring team were trying to figure out why there is a roll of toilet paper in the design of the dragon running past the duck. Are there stories behind the designs you submitted for the magazine?

Mika: We have a few ideas for upcoming publications - design sets and books - and these illustrations are from one of them. The story behind the illustrations is an old story about the monster of Lake Loukusa, a small, deep lake in northern Finland. The story about the monster is very old and has been passed down from generation to generation. The story has not (yet!) reached same level of fame as the Loch Ness Monster, though! We wanted to give the ColorOn magazine a set of high-quality coloring designs that have a common theme, and Arto proposed using these coloring designs. The book is in the pipeline and it's called A Peculiar Friendship. We hope to finalize the story and the coloring designs this year. As for the toilet paper, it's one of those funny details Arto likes to add to his designs! He thought that the first time these peculiar main characters of the story meet must be a very peculiar situation. Here the dragon is possibly emerging from the forest after, hmm, taking care of business – he certainly wouldn't soil the lake, his home! – and he bumps into the duck. A peculiar situation to start a peculiar friendship!

Color On!: How do you create your art? Do you create digitally or with pen and pencil? Tell us about your process for creating new work.

Mika: We both think about the theme of the book and the style it should have. We then generate ideas (characters, settings, scenes) for designs and Arto draws a few samples, which we discuss. Do they express the theme and idea? What kind of further development and fine-tuning is required? From there on, the artwork is pretty much Arto's area of responsibility.

When he, for example, works on these fairy-tale like illustrations, he creates a draft design with pencils to capture the idea that he has in mind. He continues sketching as long as is needed and produces version after version until he is satisfied with the end result. Sometimes the drawing flows so well that the first draft is exactly what he is looking for; at other times he needs to work on an illustration for a long time to get it just right. Once the pencil draft is ready, he starts drawing with markers (different width Micron markers, depending on the line style, and 300 gm2 high-quality drawing paper), adding details and more content as they occur to him. From time to time during the drawing process, we evaluate the designs together.

[Continued on Page 36]

As Arto is creating the art, I work on the book's name, text content, translations and publishing process. Once we have all the content in place, we put together the first draft and make decisions about the order of the designs. We want to have a certain kind of rhythm in the pictures instead of having them in just any random order. Once both Arto and I are happy, we publish the book. We are independent publishers at the moment, which gives us a lot of freedom to do things in our own way. However, we are looking for an agent to work with us to get our books published by a more heavy weight publisher.

Color On!: When coloring your own art, what is your favorite medium(s)?

Arto: I like to use aquarelle and acrylic paint with brush and airbrush. Nowadays, I do quite a lot of art and drawing with digital media, too (scanning a pencil draft and then using Photoshop.)

Mika: I love to use watercolor pencils and watercolors with brush.

Color On!: Do you enjoy relaxing with coloring books by other artists? If so, do you have a favorite artist or book?

Mika: Sadly, Arto does not have much time to color. As he works on the coloring designs on top of his daily work, there is not that much time for coloring. I did color on many different books when doing research for our first book, and would also like to find more time to color as I enjoyed it a lot. We both agree on a favorite though: it is absolutely Johanna Basford, for her line art and style. It would be very interesting to see different themed designs from her.

Color On!: What color or colors do you most love to work with?

Arto: I don't really have a favorite color; they change over time. I may have a green period, then a black one. When coloring or painting I choose a color theme, for example green. I then create a painting with different shades of green, and highlight approximately 10% of the surface by using the complementary color, in this case red. The rule of thumb is that the complementary color should cover about 10% of the area of the painting – this keeps the picture and texture interesting.

Mika: If you are asking my favorite color, I like to use black to create depth in the designs. For the colors, bright blue and deep red are perhaps my most favorite colors.

Color On!: Tell us a little bit about your art. Do you have a favorite piece that you created? Can you share some of your other artwork with us?

Mika: With our first book we wanted to create a sensual world with the ever popular garden, leaves and trees theme. We think we did well and that the level of sensuality is just right. Not too much to be explicit and downright dirty; not too little to be banal. There are a few pictures that are bit more daring, but if someone finds them a little too much there are plenty more modest ones to choose from! For the next book, Arto has further developed his drawing style to be even more flowing and artistic, and the coloring designs are drawn in A3 size. We will publish sneak peeks of our future projects on our Facebook page and blog!

In addition to coloring designs, Arto has a few other ongoing projects. One is related to Sinuhe the Egyptian, a famous Finnish historical novel by Mika Waltari, and one to the Finnish national epic Kalevala. With Sinuhe the Egyptian, the idea is to transfer the story into distant future, a bit in the style of H.R. Giger, and create a piece of art of the main characters of the novel, using acrylic paint and airbrush. These pieces have been in a few art exhibitions. In the Kalevala project Arto will also create a character gallery of the main characters. Here, he has used digital media: Cinema 3D, zBrush and Photoshop. The plan is to create a calendar with 12 character pictures. You can find Arto's illustration and art at his website www.3dart.fi.

Color On!: Who is your favorite artist or artists?

Arto: John Howe and H.R.Giger. I had the privilege of visiting Giger's art exhibition a few years ago in Tampere, Finland. There were not that many pieces on show but the artwork was amazing. Frazetta is also one of my all-time favorites. Alan Lee is excellent with aquarelle colors and did a wonderful job illustrating The Lord of the Rings. Nowadays I also check out almost every animated movie. In my opinion, the first 10 minutes of UP are top-notch fabulous. I highly recommend that everyone see the movie!

Mika: I love H.R. Giger too: the doomy and gloomy style is one of my favorites. Giger also created cover art for one of the top doom metal bands. And we must mention that Giger was the man behind the alien in the movie series Alien! Similar surrealistic, post-apocalyptic art created by Zdzisław Beksiński intrigues my darker side, too.

[Continued on Page 38]

Color On!: Is there some person, place or thing that inspires you when you are creating your art?

Arto: I'm inspired by nature. Nature and plant life produce all kinds of shapes and forms, even sensual or daring ones at times. Advertisements are also a good source for ideas: the best ads and commercials these days are true works of art. I visit art exhibitions – both figurative and abstract art – as seeing other artists' techniques and ideas is always inspiring. I also visit cgsociety.org for inspiration and new ideas.

Color On!: Other than creating coloring book art, what interesting hobbies or activities do you enjoy?

Mika: It might be easy to categorize me as business person, but I really enjoy doing things by hand. I've spent hours upon hours renovating my 1940's house: it is a never-ending project! I love beautiful things like old American classic cars, and after a 10-year break from car tinkering, I just imported a 1958 Buick Century from the US. It requires some attention and maintenance in order to be in good shape by next summer. I also build cigar box guitars – one of the ways in which my obsession for music manifests itself! I love many styles of music, from blues to the darkest heavy metal. I used to play bass in a blues band and still write songs and lyrics when time permits. In addition, I'm a board member and the treasurer of our local blues association, which organize blues gigs for local and international blues bands.

Arto: I also have a variety of interests. I like to find out about new things and enjoy reading. I'm a movie buff – cartoons in particular. I exercise a lot, going to the gym several times a week. Over the past few years, I've become passionate about cycling.

Color On!: Have you had any memorable responses to your art work from collectors?

Mika: We have been working on our social media presence and have been lucky to have people post their coloring art of our designs. Colorists seem to appreciate the style of the art in our designs very much. They find them beautiful, intriguing and flowing. However, the sensual approach is something certain people have found too much! On the other hand, others say that sensuality is THE thing they have been looking for in adult coloring designs. We thank you all who have sent us feedback and encouraging comments and are happy the designs have brought you joy!

Color On!: If each of you had to choose one superpower, what would it be?

Arto: Precognition - the ability to predict the future. I wouldn't mind knowing the lottery numbers… ;-)

Mika: Time travel would be an interesting superpower to have. It would be great to meet people like Leonardo Da Vinci, John Lee Hooker, Isaac Newton; see what nature was like 10,000 years ago; be there when the first ancestors of Finnish people arrived on Finnish ground. And be there when our first manned mission enters a new solar system out there!

Color On!: Tell us about your plans for 2016. Any other coloring books planned?

Arto: We have several book ideas! Right now, we're planning another "serious" adult coloring book. Based on what we've heard from adult colorists, we've set out to provide artistic, unique adult coloring designs for discerning adult colorist, produced on high-quality paper. We have just started work on the new book project. In order to get better funding for the project, we are planning to launch a crowdsourcing campaign.

In addition to the book project, we have ideas about a few coloring design sets that we would like to publish. The first design set, called FLOW, has been just published and is available at our Etsy shop. Depending on the time available (and naturally on how well the books sell!) there may be more books coming up during the year 2016. Together with new book projects and design set projects we will continue working to get more visibility in this very interesting but fairly crowded field of adult coloring art production.

You can learn more about Vivid Owl Coloring online.
- Full interview online: http://coloronmag.com/article/a-chat-with-vivid-owl-coloring/
- Their website: http://vividowlcoloring.com
- Their Etsy shop: https://www.etsy.com/shop/VividOwlColoring
- Their Facebook page: https://www.facebook.com/vividowlcoloring

Mika and Arto would like to thank Mari Aro for helping a lot with editing their content and language checks!

You can learn more about Vivid Owl Coloring online.

- Full interview online: http://coloronmag.com/article/a-chat-with-vivid-owl-coloring/
- Their website: http://vividowlcoloring.com
- Their Etsy shop: https://www.etsy.com/shop/VividOwlColoring
- Their Facebook page: https://www.facebook.com/vividowlcoloring

You can learn more about Vivid Owl Coloring online.
- Full interview online: http://coloronmag.com/article/a-chat-with-vivid-owl-coloring/
- Their website: http://vividowlcoloring.com
- Their Etsy shop: https://www.etsy.com/shop/VividOwlColoring
- Their Facebook page: https://www.facebook.com/vividowlcoloring

You can learn more about Vivid Owl Coloring online.

- Full interview online: http://coloronmag.com/article/a-chat-with-vivid-owl-coloring/
- Their website: http://vividowlcoloring.com
- Their Etsy shop: https://www.etsy.com/shop/VividOwlColoring
- Their Facebook page: https://www.facebook.com/vividowlcoloring

Design title: *Chidorigafuchi - Cherry Blossoms in Japan*

The vision behind the Arttapi product range was that through colouring, we could inspire adults to reconnect with their creative side and understand the importance of supporting their cognitive wellness.

The inception of this brand was created in my home office on the Northern Beaches in Sydney. I had an idea that could inspire others and even though I had never created a product before, I knew I had to follow through with my vision.

I have to give a special mention to my wonderful husband Mark who without his love and support, I could not have created such a beautiful first book. Even when I, at times, doubted if my vision could become a reality Mark's unfailing belief in me spurred me on and he never let me give up.

Launching this range of colouring books for adults and seeing my vision come to life has been greatly rewarding. I hope you will enjoy colouring the drawings as much as I have enjoyed creating them for you.

> You can learn more about Arttapi through their website:
> * Website URL: http://www.arttapi.com.au

Happy Easter

Anne Manera is an illustrator, designer and author of coloring books and children's books. Her coloring books are inspired by her paintings. Anne also runs a facebook coloring group Just Color! with Anne Manera. When she is not illustrating coloring books or hanging out with her dogs, Manera is available for painting commissions.

You can learn more about Anne online.
- Her website: http://www.annemanera.com/
- Her Facebook page: http://www.facebook.com/artbyannemaneracoloringbooks/
- Join her Facebook coloring group at http://www.facebook.com/groups/justcolorgroup

Anne Manera is an illustrator, designer and author of coloring books and children's books.Her coloring books are inspired by her paintings. Anne also runs a facebook coloring group Just Color! with Anne Manera. When she is not illustrating coloring books or hanging out with her dogs, Manera is available for painting commissions.

You can learn more about Anne online.

- Her website: http://www.annemanera.com/
- Her Facebook page: http://www.facebook.com/artbyannemaneracoloringbooks/
- Join her Facebook coloring group at http://www.facebook.com/groups/justcolorgroup

Happy Easter

Anne Manera is an illustrator, designer and author of coloring books and children's books.Her coloring books are inspired by her paintings. Anne also runs a facebook coloring group Just Color! with Anne Manera. When she is not illustrating coloring books or hanging out with her dogs, Manera is available for painting commissions.

You can learn more about Anne online.
- Her website: http://www.annemanera.com/
- Her Facebook page: http://www.facebook.com/artbyannemaneracoloringbooks/
- Join her Facebook coloring group at http://www.facebook.com/groups/justcolorgroup

Anne Manera is an illustrator, designer and author of coloring books and children's books. Her coloring books are inspired by her paintings. Anne also runs a facebook coloring group Just Color! with Anne Manera. When she is not illustrating coloring books or hanging out with her dogs, Manera is available for painting commissions.

You can learn more about Anne online.

- Her website: http://www.annemanera.com/
- Her Facebook page: http://www.facebook.com/artbyannemaneracoloringbooks/
- Join her Facebook coloring group at http://www.facebook.com/groups/justcolorgroup

Cesar Valtierra hails from the sun soaked desert of the wild, wild western city of El Paso, Texas. He wields a pencil like an outlaw gunslinger, drawing up a storm since the tender age of two. He is infamous throughout the land for his provocative ink drawings, his meticulous vector illustrations, and his eye catching graphic design work. Like a thief in the night, Mr. Valtierra is a man of few words but one who with his work makes quite an impression. He follows the beat of his own drum and answers to no one; except of course, his fiancée Victoria, the love of his life, his inspiration and muse. And their two cats, Chubs and Pretty Boy.

If you think you can handle the awesomeness, feel free to check out his work at www.cesarvaltierra.com and of course his comic book featuring the adventures of Balazo, the pint-sized detective at www.tonybalazo.com.

You can learn more about Cesar online.
- His website: http://www.cesarvaltierra.com/
- His comic – The adventures of the dapper detective Tony Balazo: http://tonybalazo.com/
- On Instagram: http://instagram.com/tonybalazo

By Dwayne
Wright

Dwayne Wright is a Native American, born to Cherokee parents. He grew up on the Indian Reservation in Cherokee, North Carolina. He left the Reservation, when he was seventeen years old, to enlist in the military during the Vietnam War. He currently works with nursing home patients and contributes his time to helping veterans. Although he is not currently a professional artist, he may pursue creating a book in the near future. He enjoys coloring with his fiancée Shelly, and finds it to be super relaxing. He volunteers to help Shelly with her Senior and Veteran projects to provide coloring books and supplies to nursing homes and VA Hospitals.

If you want to help Dwayne and Shelly with their volunteer project to provide coloring books and supplies to Seniors and Veterans, check out their Go Fund Me campaign. *Color On! Magazine* supports this project, and has an article about the Christmas donation Shelly made to the Senior Center.

- Coloring with Seniors article: http://coloronmag.com/article/coloring-with-seniors/
- https://www.gofundme.com/gjhfze2s

Gayle L. Baugh ©
8-16-2015

I was born and raised on the beautiful Mendocino Coast and spent my summers on our family ranch in Comptche, California. I went on to graduate from Mendocino Union High School and then spent some time in the San Francisco Bay area, where my daughter and son were born.

I enjoyed many years living in Clearlake, California, where working nights allowed me to expand my artistic abilities, completely self-taught. I strongly believe that my Southwestern Indian Art comes from within; inspired by my ancestors, which are traced back to the Cajun Chocktaw Indians from Louisiana.

I come from a family of Loggers and Fishermen. My passions include my family, great friends, gardening, my home, my love for animals, and of course, my art. I am now making my home, with my husband, on a little farm on the Walker River, in Yerington, Nevada.

My art is changing and evolving every day; it has opened doors that I didn't know were there!

You can learn more about Gayle's work online.

- Her website: http://gaylesfineart.com/
- Her Facebook pages:
    - http://tinyurl.com/gaylesGallery1
    - http://tinyurl.com/gaylesFineArt

HOTEL

OPEN

LOBBY

I was born and raised on the beautiful Mendocino Coast and spent my summers on our family ranch in Comptche, California. I went on to graduate from Mendocino Union High School and then spent some time in the San Francisco Bay area, where my daughter and son were born.

I enjoyed many years living in Clearlake, California, where working nights allowed me to expand my artistic abilities, completely self-taught. I strongly believe that my Southwestern Indian Art comes from within; inspired by my ancestors, which are traced back to the Cajun Chocktaw Indians from Louisiana.

I come from a family of Loggers and Fishermen. My passions include my family, great friends, gardening, my home, my love for animals, and of course, my art. I am now making my home, with my husband, on a little farm on the Walker River, in Yerington, Nevada.

My art is changing and evolving every day; it has opened doors that I didn't know were there!

You can learn more about Gayle's work online.

- Her website: http://gaylesfineart.com/
- Her Facebook pages:
    - http://tinyurl.com/gaylesGallery1
    - http://tinyurl.com/gaylesFineArt

Jason Hamilton was born in Cairo, Egypt. The son of an American father and Singaporean mother, Jason traveled the world with his parents until they returned to the US so he could attend high school and college. His two great interests were art and computers. He so excelled in art his high school hired a special art teacher just to encourage his talents. However, the lure of computers was greater. He majored in Computer Science in college and went on to a career as a software engineer with AT&T and Verizon.

When a good friend asked him to sketch a few pictures for her to color while undergoing dialysis, Jason picked her two favorite subjects and combined her love for cats and quilts into a series of illustrations.

Amazon's CreateSpace has published of some of these illustrations in *Cats & Quilts*. Jason hopes it brings peace, love, and warmth to colorists of all ages and abilities. Jason has since continued to create other coloring books.

You can learn more about Jason's work online.

- His website: http://www.bluecatgallery.com
- His books on Amazon: http://tinyurl.com/jasonColoring

bluecatgallery.com

Jason Hamilton was born in Cairo, Egypt. The son of an American father and Singaporean mother, Jason traveled the world with his parents until they returned to the US so he could attend high school and college. His two great interests were art and computers. He so excelled in art his high school hired a special art teacher just to encourage his talents. However, the lure of computers was greater. He majored in Computer Science in college and went on to a career as a software engineer with AT&T and Verizon.

When a good friend asked him to sketch a few pictures for her to color while undergoing dialysis, Jason picked her two favorite subjects and combined her love for cats and quilts into a series of illustrations.

Amazon's CreateSpace has published of some of these illustrations in *Cats & Quilts*. Jason hopes it brings peace, love, and warmth to colorists of all ages and abilities. Jason has since continued to create other coloring books.

You can learn more about Jason's work online.

- His website: http://www.bluecatgallery.com
- His books on Amazon: http://tinyurl.com/jasonColoring

I have always enjoyed working with ink, and started expressing interest in drawing around 10 years of age. As the years passed, I found sketching and drawing to be fairly easy. It's always been a favorite hobby of mine, and a great way to relieve stress. As I approached my mid 20's, I began to thoroughly develop my own art style and have perfected it over the past 30 or so years. Now that I am entering over five decades of age, I have saved hundreds of unique artworks that could be considered surreal, which I would consider to be "the Broken Mind of Joe's Ink."

One particular occasion that pushed me to develop such original art was my high school art teacher. Having not yet delved into my unique style, I was told that I had no imagination whatsoever. That message taunted me subconsciously and lead to the creation of the one of a kind work that you see today.

You can find Joe online.

- His Facebook page: http://tinyurl.com/BrokenMindOfJoesInk
- Payhip site: https://payhip.com/joesinkearthlinknet
- His books on Amazon: http://tinyurl.com/JoesInkBooks

I have always enjoyed working with ink, and started expressing interest in drawing around 10 years of age. As the years passed, I found sketching and drawing to be fairly easy. It's always been a favorite hobby of mine, and a great way to relieve stress. As I approached my mid 20's, I began to thoroughly develop my own art style and have perfected it over the past 30 or so years. Now that I am entering over five decades of age, I have saved hundreds of unique artworks that could be considered surreal, which I would consider to be "the Broken Mind of Joe's Ink."

One particular occasion that pushed me to develop such original art was my high school art teacher. Having not yet delved into my unique style, I was told that I had no imagination whatsoever. That message taunted me subconsciously and lead to the creation of the one of a kind work that you see today.

> You can find Joe online.
>
> - His Facebook page: http://tinyurl.com/BrokenMindOfJoesInk
> - Payhip site: https://payhip.com/joesinkearthlinknet
> - His books on Amazon: http://tinyurl.com/JoesInkBooks

Although my educational background is far from the artistic domain, in the last years, I have pushed myself to express my inner impulse towards the Arts. I suddenly started to paint in December 2001, and I feel I will never stop. I have never taken art classes to learn nor have I asked a professional about my works.

I was only following a need to express myself, a need to find a way in this world, a need to discover new things.

These years of exploration have given me a lot; they give me ideas about this universe of shapes and colors around us. They also give me more than this, since it gives me great pleasure to create, a pleasure to live. Art gives me a reason for being in this world.

You can learn more about Julian's works online:

- His website: http://juliantrocaru.com
- His book on Amazon: http://tinyurl.com/trocaru

Although my educational background is far from the artistic domain, in the last years, I have pushed myself to express my inner impulse towards the Arts. I suddenly started to paint in December 2001, and I feel I will never stop. I have never taken art classes to learn nor have I asked a professional about my works.

I was only following a need to express myself, a need to find a way in this world, a need to discover new things.

These years of exploration have given me a lot; they give me ideas about this universe of shapes and colors around us. They also give me more than this, since it gives me great pleasure to create, a pleasure to live. Art gives me a reason for being in this world.

You can learn more about Julian's works online:

- His website: http://juliantrocaru.com
- His book on Amazon: http://tinyurl.com/trocaru

BLARF THE
BULLET CHERUB

Design title: *Blarf the Bullet Cherub*

You can find more work by Karlon at http://blackriverart.com

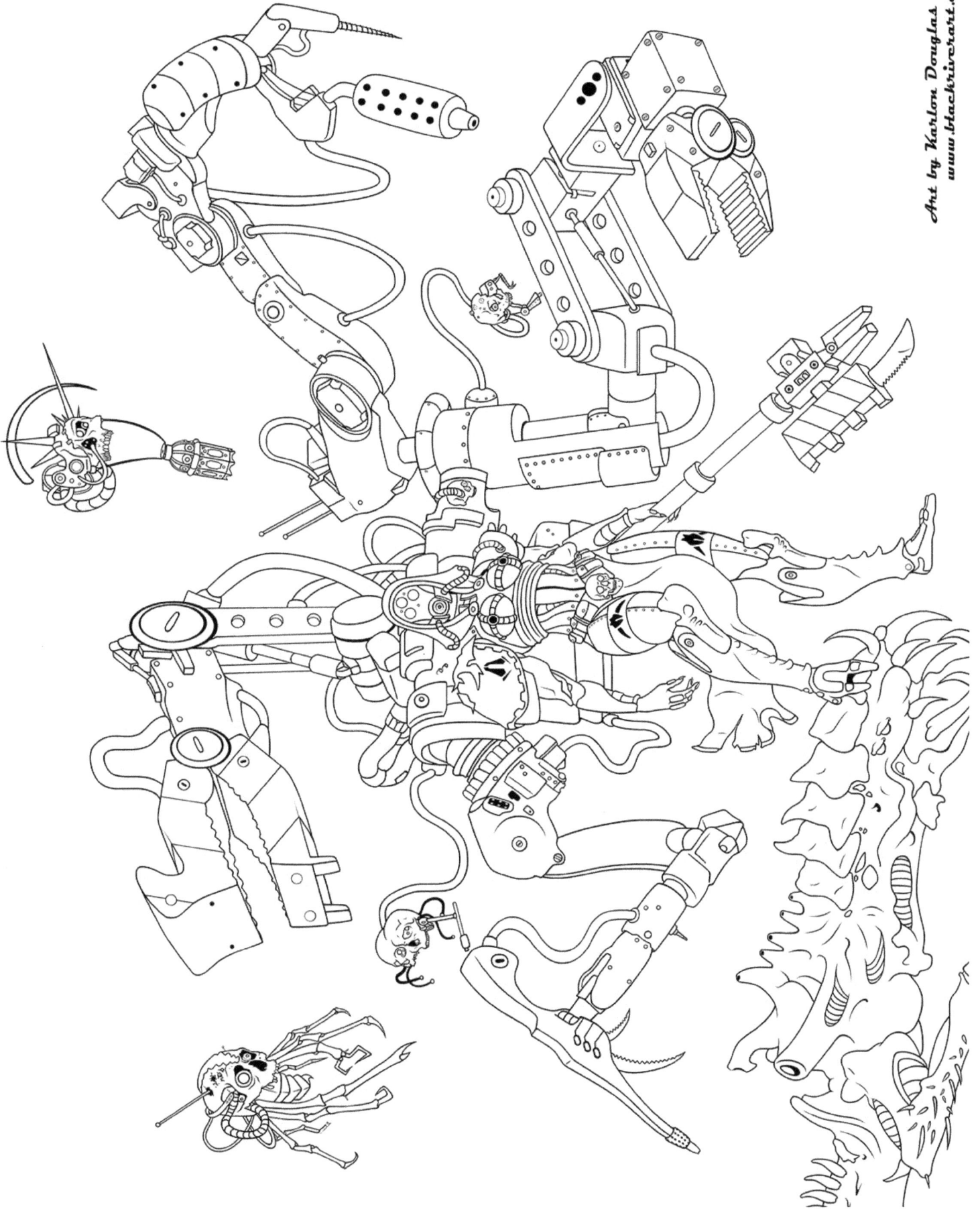

Design title: *Warhammer Tali Zorah*

You can find more work by Karlon at http://blackriverart.com

Tattoo artist Komfort Wiafe has decided to share her amazing art for colorists to enjoy. Color with Komfort is her new coloring book series, with *Mind's Eye of a Gypsy* as the first book, available now on Amazon.

> You can find Komfort's current book, plus any future books she publishes, using this link:
>
> - Books on Amazon: http://tinyurl.com/KomfortWiafeBooks

Tattoo artist Komfort Wiafe has decided to share her amazing art for colorists to enjoy. Color with Komfort is her new coloring book series, with *Mind's Eye of a Gypsy* as the first book, available now on Amazon.

You can find Komfort's current book, plus any future books she publishes, using this link:

- Books on Amazon: http://tinyurl.com/KomfortWiafeBooks

Tattoo artist Komfort Wiafe has decided to share her amazing art for colorists to enjoy. Color with Komfort is her new coloring book series, with *Mind's Eye of a Gypsy* as the first book, available now on Amazon.

You can find Komfort's current book, plus any future books she publishes, using this link:

- Books on Amazon: http://tinyurl.com/KomfortWiafeBooks

Design title: *Time Warp*

Mary J. Winters-Meyer has been a creative since she was a child, but didn't consider herself an "artist" until she was in her 30s. Her first professional artistic adventure was in the world of bead weaving, where she had some success, winning several awards for her artwork, having an article published in *Bead & Button*, and self-publishing a bead pattern book. Her "real job" designing websites kept her from pursuing an artistic career at that time, keeping her busy for over 15 years.

In 2013, Mary started drawing her mandala-inspired artwork with science fiction and fantasy themes. That art eventually led to her foray into the coloring world, and in 2015 she began exploring that world full time. Her Facebook group, Coloring Books for Adults, has been tremendously successful, gaining over 30,000 members in less than a year. Members enjoy posting their colored works and sharing their passion for coloring in a positive atmosphere.

Additionally, Mary hosts a coloring review blog, also titled Coloring Books for Adults. The site features both written and video reviews of coloring books and products. Her reviews are also included in *Color On! Magazine*.

In October 2015, Mary launched *Color On! Magazine*. The magazine is now available both as a digital subscription and a full color printed issue, with both articles and coloring pages for colorists to enjoy. Print anthologies like this one are also published every three months, with the designs from the three magazine issues.

You can learn more about Mary online:
- Join Mary's Facebook group at https://www.facebook.com/groups/ColoringBooksForAdults
- Coloring Books for Adults review blog: http://AdultColoringBooks.com
- *Color On! Magazine*: http://ColorOnMag.com
- *Color On! Magazine* Facebook page: https://www.facebook.com/ColorOnMag
- *Color On! Magazine* Etsy shop: http://www.etsy.com/shop/ColorOnMagazine
- Mary's artwork for sale: http://tangitude.com
- Mary's books on Amazon: http://tinyurl.com/Tangitude

猴
2016

Design title: *2016 – Year of Monkey Business*

Mary J. Winters-Meyer has been a creative since she was a child, but didn't consider herself an "artist" until she was in her 30s. Her first professional artistic adventure was in the world of bead weaving, where she had some success, winning several awards for her artwork, having an article published in *Bead & Button*, and self-publishing a bead pattern book. Her "real job" designing websites kept her from pursuing an artistic career at that time, keeping her busy for over 15 years.

In 2013, Mary started drawing her mandala-inspired artwork with science fiction and fantasy themes. That art eventually led to her foray into the coloring world, and in 2015 she began exploring that world full time. Her Facebook group, Coloring Books for Adults, has been tremendously successful, gaining over 30,000 members in less than a year. Members enjoy posting their colored works and sharing their passion for coloring in a positive atmosphere.

Additionally, Mary hosts a coloring review blog, also titled Coloring Books for Adults. The site features both written and video reviews of coloring books and products. Her reviews are also included in *Color On! Magazine*.

In October 2015, Mary launched *Color On! Magazine*. The magazine is now available both as a digital subscription and a full color printed issue, with both articles and coloring pages for colorists to enjoy. Print anthologies like this one are also published every three months, with the designs from the three magazine issues.

You can learn more about Mary online:
- Join Mary's Facebook group at https://www.facebook.com/groups/ColoringBooksForAdults
- Coloring Books for Adults review blog: http://AdultColoringBooks.com
- *Color On! Magazine*: http://ColorOnMag.com
- *Color On! Magazine* Facebook page: https://www.facebook.com/ColorOnMag
- *Color On! Magazine* Etsy shop: http://www.etsy.com/shop/ColorOnMagazine
- Mary's artwork for sale: http://tangitude.com
- Mary's books on Amazon: http://tinyurl.com/Tangitude

Mary J. Winters-Meyer has been a creative since she was a child, but didn't consider herself an "artist" until she was in her 30s. Her first professional artistic adventure was in the world of bead weaving, where she had some success, winning several awards for her artwork, having an article published in *Bead & Button*, and self-publishing a bead pattern book. Her "real job" designing websites kept her from pursuing an artistic career at that time, keeping her busy for over 15 years.

In 2013, Mary started drawing her mandala-inspired artwork with science fiction and fantasy themes. That art eventually led to her foray into the coloring world, and in 2015 she began exploring that world full time. Her Facebook group, Coloring Books for Adults, has been tremendously successful, gaining over 30,000 members in less than a year. Members enjoy posting their colored works and sharing their passion for coloring in a positive atmosphere.

Additionally, Mary hosts a coloring review blog, also titled Coloring Books for Adults. The site features both written and video reviews of coloring books and products. Her reviews are also included in *Color On! Magazine*.

In October 2015, Mary launched *Color On! Magazine*. The magazine is now available both as a digital subscription and a full color printed issue, with both articles and coloring pages for colorists to enjoy. Print anthologies like this one are also published every three months, with the designs from the three magazine issues.

You can learn more about Mary online:
- Join Mary's Facebook group at https://www.facebook.com/groups/ColoringBooksForAdults
- Coloring Books for Adults review blog: http://AdultColoringBooks.com
- *Color On! Magazine*: http://ColorOnMag.com
- *Color On! Magazine* Facebook page: https://www.facebook.com/ColorOnMag
- *Color On! Magazine* Etsy shop: http://www.etsy.com/shop/ColorOnMagazine
- Mary's artwork for sale: http://tangitude.com
- Mary's books on Amazon: http://tinyurl.com/Tangitude

Design title: *March Hare*

Mary J. Winters-Meyer has been a creative since she was a child, but didn't consider herself an "artist" until she was in her 30s. Her first professional artistic adventure was in the world of bead weaving, where she had some success, winning several awards for her artwork, having an article published in *Bead & Button*, and self-publishing a bead pattern book. Her "real job" designing websites kept her from pursuing an artistic career at that time, keeping her busy for over 15 years.

In 2013, Mary started drawing her mandala-inspired artwork with science fiction and fantasy themes. That art eventually led to her foray into the coloring world, and in 2015 she began exploring that world full time. Her Facebook group, Coloring Books for Adults, has been tremendously successful, gaining over 30,000 members in less than a year. Members enjoy posting their colored works and sharing their passion for coloring in a positive atmosphere.

Additionally, Mary hosts a coloring review blog, also titled Coloring Books for Adults. The site features both written and video reviews of coloring books and products. Her reviews are also included in *Color On! Magazine*.

In October 2015, Mary launched *Color On! Magazine*. The magazine is now available both as a digital subscription and a full color printed issue, with both articles and coloring pages for colorists to enjoy. Print anthologies like this one are also published every three months, with the designs from the three magazine issues.

You can learn more about Mary online:
- Join Mary's Facebook group at https://www.facebook.com/groups/ColoringBooksForAdults
- Coloring Books for Adults review blog: http://AdultColoringBooks.com
- *Color On! Magazine*: http://ColorOnMag.com
- *Color On! Magazine* Facebook page: https://www.facebook.com/ColorOnMag
- *Color On! Magazine* Etsy shop: http://www.etsy.com/shop/ColorOnMagazine
- Mary's artwork for sale: http://tangitude.com
- Mary's books on Amazon: http://tinyurl.com/Tangitude

Design title: *Celtic Flower*

Mary J. Winters-Meyer has been a creative since she was a child, but didn't consider herself an "artist" until she was in her 30s. Her first professional artistic adventure was in the world of bead weaving, where she had some success, winning several awards for her artwork, having an article published in *Bead & Button*, and self-publishing a bead pattern book. Her "real job" designing websites kept her from pursuing an artistic career at that time, keeping her busy for over 15 years.

In 2013, Mary started drawing her mandala-inspired artwork with science fiction and fantasy themes. That art eventually led to her foray into the coloring world, and in 2015 she began exploring that world full time. Her Facebook group, Coloring Books for Adults, has been tremendously successful, gaining over 30,000 members in less than a year. Members enjoy posting their colored works and sharing their passion for coloring in a positive atmosphere.

Additionally, Mary hosts a coloring review blog, also titled Coloring Books for Adults. The site features both written and video reviews of coloring books and products. Her reviews are also included in *Color On! Magazine*.

In October 2015, Mary launched *Color On! Magazine.* The magazine is now available both as a digital subscription and a full color printed issue, with both articles and coloring pages for colorists to enjoy. Print anthologies like this one are also published every three months, with the designs from the three magazine issues.

You can learn more about Mary online:
- Join Mary's Facebook group at https://www.facebook.com/groups/ColoringBooksForAdults
- Coloring Books for Adults review blog: http://AdultColoringBooks.com
- *Color On! Magazine*: http://ColorOnMag.com
- *Color On! Magazine* Facebook page: https://www.facebook.com/ColorOnMag
- *Color On! Magazine* Etsy shop: http://www.etsy.com/shop/ColorOnMagazine
- Mary's artwork for sale: http://tangitude.com
- Mary's books on Amazon: http://tinyurl.com/Tangitude

Mary J. Winters-Meyer has been a creative since she was a child, but didn't consider herself an "artist" until she was in her 30s. Her first professional artistic adventure was in the world of bead weaving, where she had some success, winning several awards for her artwork, having an article published in *Bead & Button*, and self-publishing a bead pattern book. Her "real job" designing websites kept her from pursuing an artistic career at that time, keeping her busy for over 15 years.

In 2013, Mary started drawing her mandala-inspired artwork with science fiction and fantasy themes. That art eventually led to her foray into the coloring world, and in 2015 she began exploring that world full time. Her Facebook group, Coloring Books for Adults, has been tremendously successful, gaining over 30,000 members in less than a year. Members enjoy posting their colored works and sharing their passion for coloring in a positive atmosphere.

Additionally, Mary hosts a coloring review blog, also titled Coloring Books for Adults. The site features both written and video reviews of coloring books and products. Her reviews are also included in *Color On! Magazine*.

In October 2015, Mary launched *Color On! Magazine*. The magazine is now available both as a digital subscription and a full color printed issue, with both articles and coloring pages for colorists to enjoy. Print anthologies like this one are also published every three months, with the designs from the three magazine issues.

You can learn more about Mary online:
- Join Mary's Facebook group at https://www.facebook.com/groups/ColoringBooksForAdults
- Coloring Books for Adults review blog: http://AdultColoringBooks.com
- *Color On! Magazine*: http://ColorOnMag.com
- *Color On! Magazine* Facebook page: https://www.facebook.com/ColorOnMag
- *Color On! Magazine* Etsy shop: http://www.etsy.com/shop/ColorOnMagazine
- Mary's artwork for sale: http://tangitude.com
- Mary's books on Amazon: http://tinyurl.com/Tangitude

Olivia Julius Dunggat

Design title: *Bujang senang*

Malaysia-based illustrator Olivia Julius Dunggat is a self-taught artist who believes that art should be for everyone, and everyone can create art. She works mainly with black fineliners to illustrate whimsical tribal doodles and designs. She draws inspiration from the vibrant and rich cultural background of her tribe, Iban of Sarawak (Malaysia Borneo). Her *Sarawak Tattoo Mandalas* coloring book for adults contains beautifully illustrated mandalas inspired by Sarawak tribal tattoo motifs. Olivia lives and works in Kuching, Sarawak and currently she is working on her second coloring book for adults, *Be Encouraged! Inspirational Quotes.*

You can learn more about Olivia online:
- Her website: http://coloringiship.com/
- Her Etsy shop: https://www.etsy.com/shop/ColoringIsHip
- Her Instagram: https://www.instagram.com/coloringiship/
- Her Facebook page: https://facebook.com/coloringiship/

Olivia Julius Dunggat

Design title: *Bungai terung*

Malaysia-based illustrator Olivia Julius Dunggat is a self-taught artist who believes that art should be for everyone, and everyone can create art. She works mainly with black fineliners to illustrate whimsical tribal doodles and designs. She draws inspiration from the vibrant and rich cultural background of her tribe, Iban of Sarawak (Malaysia Borneo). Her *Sarawak Tattoo Mandalas* coloring book for adults contains beautifully illustrated mandalas inspired by Sarawak tribal tattoo motifs. Olivia lives and works in Kuching, Sarawak and currently she is working on her second coloring book for adults, *Be Encouraged! Inspirational Quotes.*

You can learn more about Olivia online:
- Her website: http://coloringiship.com/
- Her Etsy shop: https://www.etsy.com/shop/ColoringIsHip
- Her Instagram: https://www.instagram.com/coloringiship/
- Her Facebook page: https://facebook.com/coloringiship/

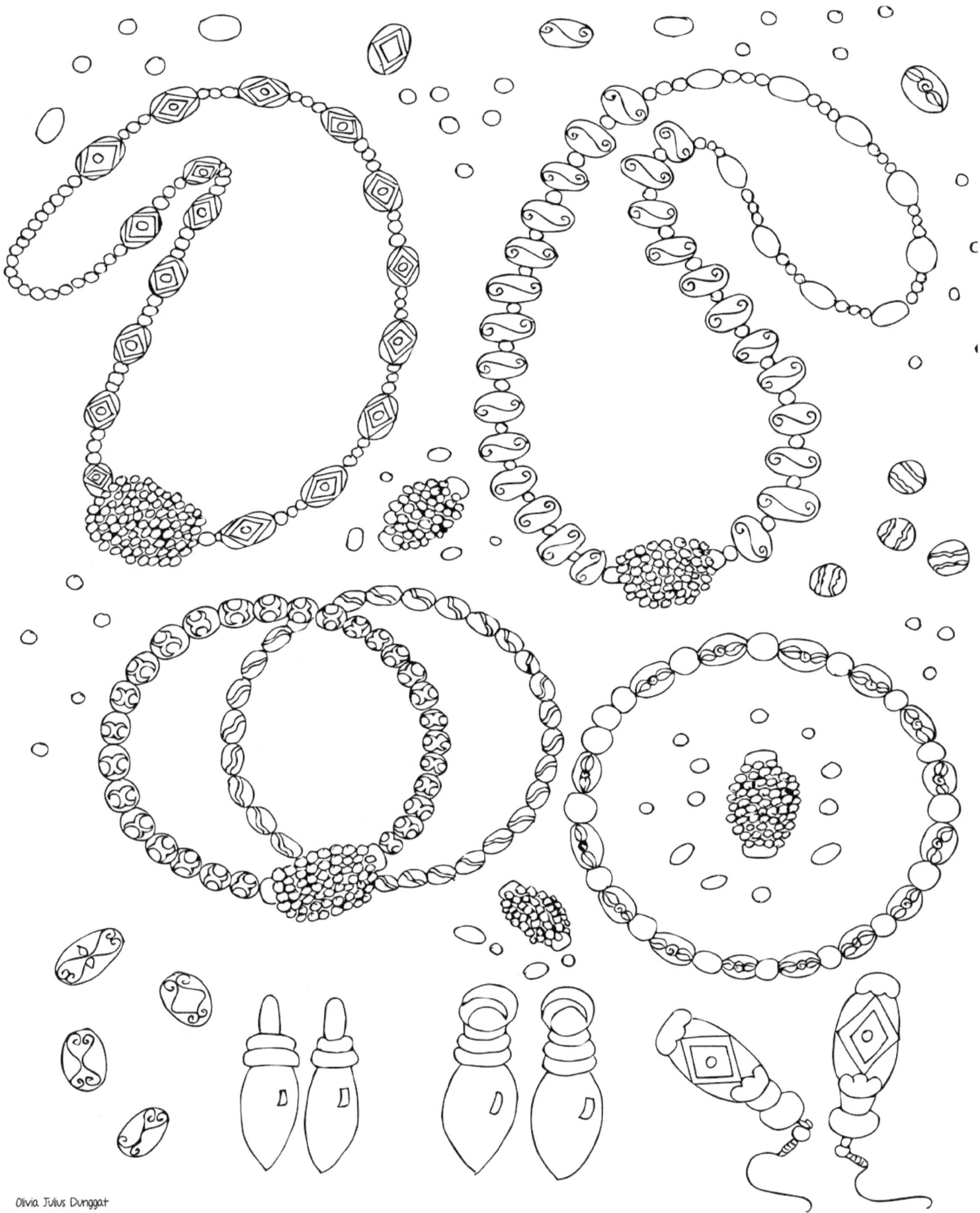

Olivia Julius Dunggat

Design title: *Orang ulu beads*

Malaysia-based illustrator Olivia Julius Dunggat is a self-taught artist who believes that art should be for everyone, and everyone can create art. She works mainly with black fineliners to illustrate whimsical tribal doodles and designs. She draws inspiration from the vibrant and rich cultural background of her tribe, Iban of Sarawak (Malaysia Borneo). Her *Sarawak Tattoo Mandalas* coloring book for adults contains beautifully illustrated mandalas inspired by Sarawak tribal tattoo motifs. Olivia lives and works in Kuching, Sarawak and currently she is working on her second coloring book for adults, *Be Encouraged! Inspirational Quotes.*

You can learn more about Olivia online:
- Her website: http://coloringiship.com/
- Her Etsy shop: https://www.etsy.com/shop/ColoringIsHip
- Her Instagram: https://www.instagram.com/coloringiship/
- Her Facebook page: https://facebook.com/coloringiship/

Design title: *Tribal motif*

Malaysia-based illustrator Olivia Julius Dunggat is a self-taught artist who believes that art should be for everyone, and everyone can create art. She works mainly with black fineliners to illustrate whimsical tribal doodles and designs. She draws inspiration from the vibrant and rich cultural background of her tribe, Iban of Sarawak (Malaysia Borneo). Her *Sarawak Tattoo Mandalas* coloring book for adults contains beautifully illustrated mandalas inspired by Sarawak tribal tattoo motifs. Olivia lives and works in Kuching, Sarawak and currently she is working on her second coloring book for adults, *Be Encouraged! Inspirational Quotes*.

You can learn more about Olivia online:
- Her website: http://coloringiship.com/
- Her Etsy shop: https://www.etsy.com/shop/ColoringIsHip
- Her Instagram: https://www.instagram.com/coloringiship/
- Her Facebook page: https://facebook.com/coloringiship/

HEARTS COLORING BOOK
PENNY FARTHING GRAPHICS

Penny Farthing Graphics has been publishing adult coloring books since 2013.

We publish both original designs as well as high quality, hand-curated licensed images from artists around the world.

In all of our coloring books for grown-ups we try and provide a wide range of styles and difficulty levels so they can be enjoyed by novices as well as advanced adult colorists.

You can learn more about Penny Farthing Graphics online:
- Facebook page: https://www.facebook.com/pennyfarthingcoloringbooks
- Books on Amazon: http://tinyurl.com/AmznPennyFarthing

Penny Farthing Graphics has been publishing adult coloring books since 2013.

We publish both original designs as well as high quality, hand-curated licensed images from artists around the world.

In all of our coloring books for grown-ups we try and provide a wide range of styles and difficulty levels so they can be enjoyed by novices as well as advanced adult colorists.

> You can learn more about Penny Farthing Graphics online:
> - Facebook page: https://www.facebook.com/pennyfarthingcoloringbooks
> - Books on Amazon: http://tinyurl.com/AmznPennyFarthing

Penny Farthing Graphics has been publishing adult coloring books since 2013.

We publish both original designs as well as high quality, hand-curated licensed images from artists around the world.

In all of our coloring books for grown-ups we try and provide a wide range of styles and difficulty levels so they can be enjoyed by novices as well as advanced adult colorists.

You can learn more about Penny Farthing Graphics online:
- Facebook page: https://www.facebook.com/pennyfarthingcoloringbooks
- Books on Amazon: http://tinyurl.com/AmznPennyFarthing

Designer of over 100 theatrical productions, Rick St Dennis is also the author of four books on decorative painting, and contributor to at least a dozen national magazines on crafts and art. He has taught design at the college level as well as seminars and classes across the USA and Canada. He is one of a handful of designers to have designed TWO productions of AIDA, Verdi's massive Egyptian opera spectacle.

Currently living in the quiet beach community of Seal Beach, California, he writes restaurant reviews and theatre reviews between assignments for web designs, logos and creating art for local shows. Rick has appeared on such TV shows as Home Matters with Susan Powell, Aileen's Crafts and others. He was Crafts editor for Country Folk Art Magazine, and sells his artwork nationally through galleries and shows.

Among numerous awards he won a presidential commendation in 1976 for his contributions to the bicentennial year including the design of the west coast premiere of William Grant Still's opera BAYOU LEGEND. His drawings and paintings are in the collections of Diana Ross, Sandy Duncan, Sammy Davis Jr. and Jacqueline Onassis amongst others.

You can learn more about Rick online:
- Rick's blog: http://rickstdennis.blogspot.com
- His Facebook page: https://www.facebook.com/profile.php?id=100001352417852
- His Etsy shop: https://www.etsy.com/shop/RickStdennis
- His Zibbet shop (similar to Etsy): https://www.zibbet.com/rick1949

Designer of over 100 theatrical productions, Rick St Dennis is also the author of four books on decorative painting, and contributor to at least a dozen national magazines on crafts and art. He has taught design at the college level as well as seminars and classes across the USA and Canada. He is one of a handful of designers to have designed TWO productions of AIDA, Verdi's massive Egyptian opera spectacle.

Currently living in the quiet beach community of Seal Beach, California, he writes restaurant reviews and theatre reviews between assignments for web designs, logos and creating art for local shows. Rick has appeared on such TV shows as Home Matters with Susan Powell, Aileen's Crafts and others. He was Crafts editor for Country Folk Art Magazine, and sells his artwork nationally through galleries and shows.

Among numerous awards he won a presidential commendation in 1976 for his contributions to the bicentennial year including the design of the west coast premiere of William Grant Still's opera BAYOU LEGEND. His drawings and paintings are in the collections of Diana Ross, Sandy Duncan, Sammy Davis Jr. and Jacqueline Onassis amongst others.

You can learn more about Rick online:
- Rick's blog: http://rickstdennis.blogspot.com
- His Facebook page: https://www.facebook.com/profile.php?id=100001352417852
- His Etsy shop: https://www.etsy.com/shop/RickStdennis
- His Zibbet shop (similar to Etsy): https://www.zibbet.com/rick1949

Sena Carroz lives in Missouri with her husband, two dogs, two cats and one parrot named Captain Jack. She has loved all things art related since she was little – coloring being a big one she never grew out of. She can usually be found in her favorite chair reading, or doodling some sketches.

You can purchase Sena's lovely art in her coloring book, available on Amazon:

- *The Mermaids Lounge:* http://amzn.to/25233t4

Sena Carroz lives in Missouri with her husband, two dogs, two cats and one parrot named Captain Jack. She has loved all things art related since she was little – coloring being a big one she never grew out of. She can usually be found in her favorite chair reading, or doodling some sketches.

You can purchase Sena's lovely art in her coloring book, available on Amazon:

* *The Mermaids Lounge:* http://amzn.to/25233t4

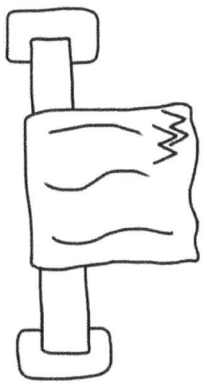

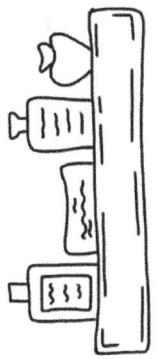

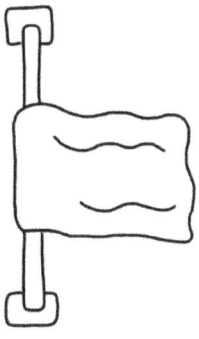

Tracey is working on her first coloring book, which may be available by the time you get this anthology. You can read more about the book on her Facebook page at https://www.facebook.com/narwhalidays.

Tracey is working on her first coloring book, which may be available by the time you get this anthology. You can read more about the book on her Facebook page at https://www.facebook.com/narwhalidays.

Valerie Jagiello – fine artist, graphic designer and photographer

Valerie was a child prodigy who started to draw the first day she picked up a Crayola...and has never stopped. All of her formal education was in New York City. For several years after school she worked in Advertising as both a creative and art director but left Madison Avenue because she didn't like being creative "on demand". Valerie left the nine to five world and never looked back!

A keen observer of life and the world around her Valerie is constantly looking for new sources or products to use within the creative process. Everyday you can find her in the studio, which she shares with Harry and the Fisch, creating something. Even now, at times...she still uses her Crayolas.

Nocturnal by choice...Valerie prefers to work at night when most of the world is still.

During her lifetime Valerie has won numerous awards and has had many shows. These are unimportant....as art and creating art are her reasons for being. "I am a working artist...who is blessed creating what I like. I will continue to work until the day I die"!!!

HARRY Gareth Edward Spaulding - muse, writer and artist

Harry came into Valerie's life several years ago as a rescue Pulik from Birmingham, UK (with a brief stopover in New Jersey). With his beautiful soul and wonderful spirit he quickly became Valerie's muse and the two were never apart. Between modelling projects for his Mum and his job as a Puli at large reporter, he started gathering his own thoughts and ideas for creating his own line of children's books... and now focuses on coloring books.

Allister FISCHER Edward Spaulding III (the Fisch) – muse II, writer and artist

The Fisch joined the group about three years ago and the fit was perfect. Fisch was a rescue Puli too...but from Oklahoma City. He's the jester of the group... and also models with "older" brother Harry for his Mum when needed. He fills the rest of his time getting belly rubs which is his number one fav activity, writing and working on his other artistic projects.

> You can learn more about Valerie, Harry and the Fisch online:
> - *Color On!* interview: http://coloronmag.com/article/a-chat-with-valerie-harry-the-fisch
> - Her Facebook page at https://www.facebook.com/Valerie-Harry-the-Fisch-1644859139128874
> - The write your own story website at http://www.ColorYourStory.com
> - The write your own story product store at http://www.coloryourstory-thestore.com
> - Valerie's photography at http://fineartamerica.com/profiles/valerie-jagiello.html

2016 Valerie, Harry & the Fisch

Valerie Jagiello – fine artist, graphic designer and photographer

Valerie was a child prodigy who started to draw the first day she picked up a Crayola...and has never stopped. All of her formal education was in New York City. For several years after school she worked in Advertising as both a creative and art director but left Madison Avenue because she didn't like being creative "on demand". Valerie left the nine to five world and never looked back!

A keen observer of life and the world around her Valerie is constantly looking for new sources or products to use within the creative process. Everyday you can find her in the studio, which she shares with Harry and the Fisch, creating something. Even now, at times...she still uses her Crayolas.

Nocturnal by choice...Valerie prefers to work at night when most of the world is still.

During her lifetime Valerie has won numerous awards and has had many shows. These are unimportant....as art and creating art are her reasons for being. "I am a working artist...who is blessed creating what I like. I will continue to work until the day I die"!!!

HARRY Gareth Edward Spaulding - muse, writer and artist

Harry came into Valerie's life several years ago as a rescue Pulik from Birmingham, UK (with a brief stopover in New Jersey). With his beautiful soul and wonderful spirit he quickly became Valerie's muse and the two were never apart. Between modelling projects for his Mum and his job as a Puli at large reporter, he started gathering his own thoughts and ideas for creating his own line of children's books... and now focuses on coloring books.

Allister FISCHER Edward Spaulding III (the Fisch) – muse II, writer and artist

The Fisch joined the group about three years ago and the fit was perfect. Fisch was a rescue Puli too...but from Oklahoma City. He's the jester of the group... and also models with "older" brother Harry for his Mum when needed. He fills the rest of his time getting belly rubs which is his number one fav activity, writing and working on his other artistic projects.

You can learn more about Valerie, Harry and the Fisch online:
- *Color On!* interview: http://coloronmag.com/article/a-chat-with-valerie-harry-the-fisch
- Her Facebook page at https://www.facebook.com/Valerie-Harry-the-Fisch-1644859139128874
- The write your own story website at http://www.ColorYourStory.com
- The write your own story product store at http://www.coloryourstory-thestore.com
- Valerie's photography at http://fineartamerica.com/profiles/valerie-jagiello.html

The name is VALPYRA!

VALPYRA SKULLSTYR....MASTER Grim Reaper artist and digital manipulator who appreciates the Dark Arts and embraces the Goth lifestyle.

A child prodigy and experimental artist, Valpyra's affinity for the dark arts (both visual and written) began during the first days of middle school. The metamorphosis began.

All of her formal education took place in New York City. While in college she subsidized herself and her art by being a model. Valpyra met many artists, illustrators and photographers who have remained friends. During this time, she partnered with illustrator...norm eastman and opened a photographic studio. For the next few years they worked together but closed their New York studio to travel and pursue solo careers.

Today, she prefers a more solitary lifestyle living near Death Valley. It is here she can truly be herself and totally focus on her work. Valpyra shares Skullstyr, an old stone building with Igor...a very opinionated raven and Sasha...a wolf hybrid.

Valpyra was born to observe and create through her work. She stirs feelings, fuels the fires of desire and evokes a primal reaction within each viewer. These are the forces which drive her as an artist!

"I weave a lot of reds through out my work. RED is the color of passion, life and blood!"

"My latest work is a new form of cerebral aesthetic Cubism on many different visual levels. This digital expression of a "multiple view" subject is similar to work created by Picasso, and the patterned works of Gustav Klimt. Textures, shapes, colors, lights and motion are all key segments in building the creative foundation found in each illustration or print."

Valpyra uses a vast collection of filters, interacting masks and textures when creating new art. This final visual statement challenges the viewer....while testing their senses.

VALPYRA is now incorporating most of these techniques into her coloring images and themed coloring books!

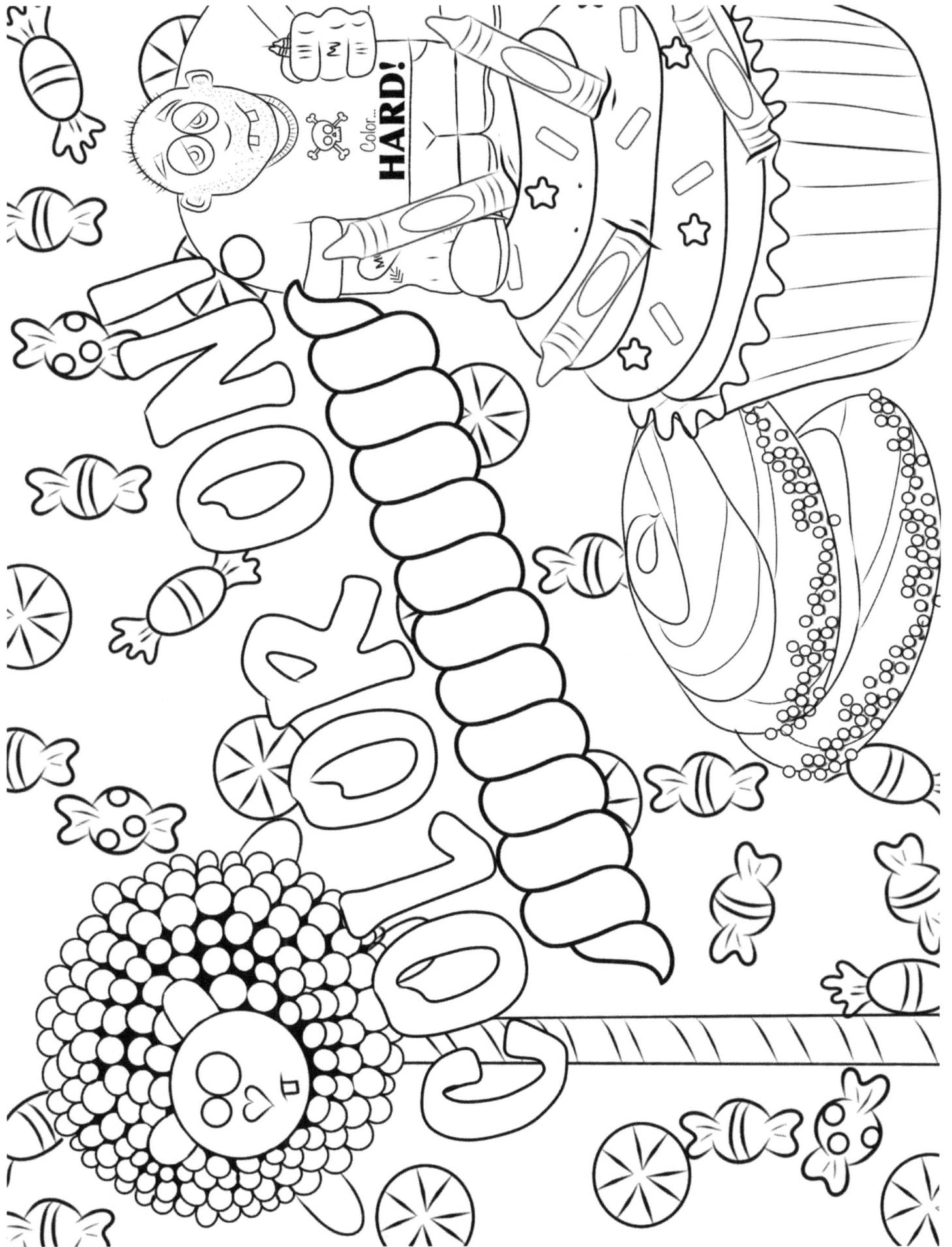

Color... **HARD!**

ENJOY
YOUR
LIFE

You can learn more about J.A. Early Riser & T.J. Crayons online.

- Full interview online: http://coloronmag.com/article/a-chat-with-absurdians-j-a-early-riser-and-t-j-crayons/
- Their website: http://maniacalconfessions.com
- Their Etsy shop: https://www.etsy.com/shop/ManiacalConfessions
- Join the Weirdos Facebook group: https://www.facebook.com/groups/ColoUringForWeirdos

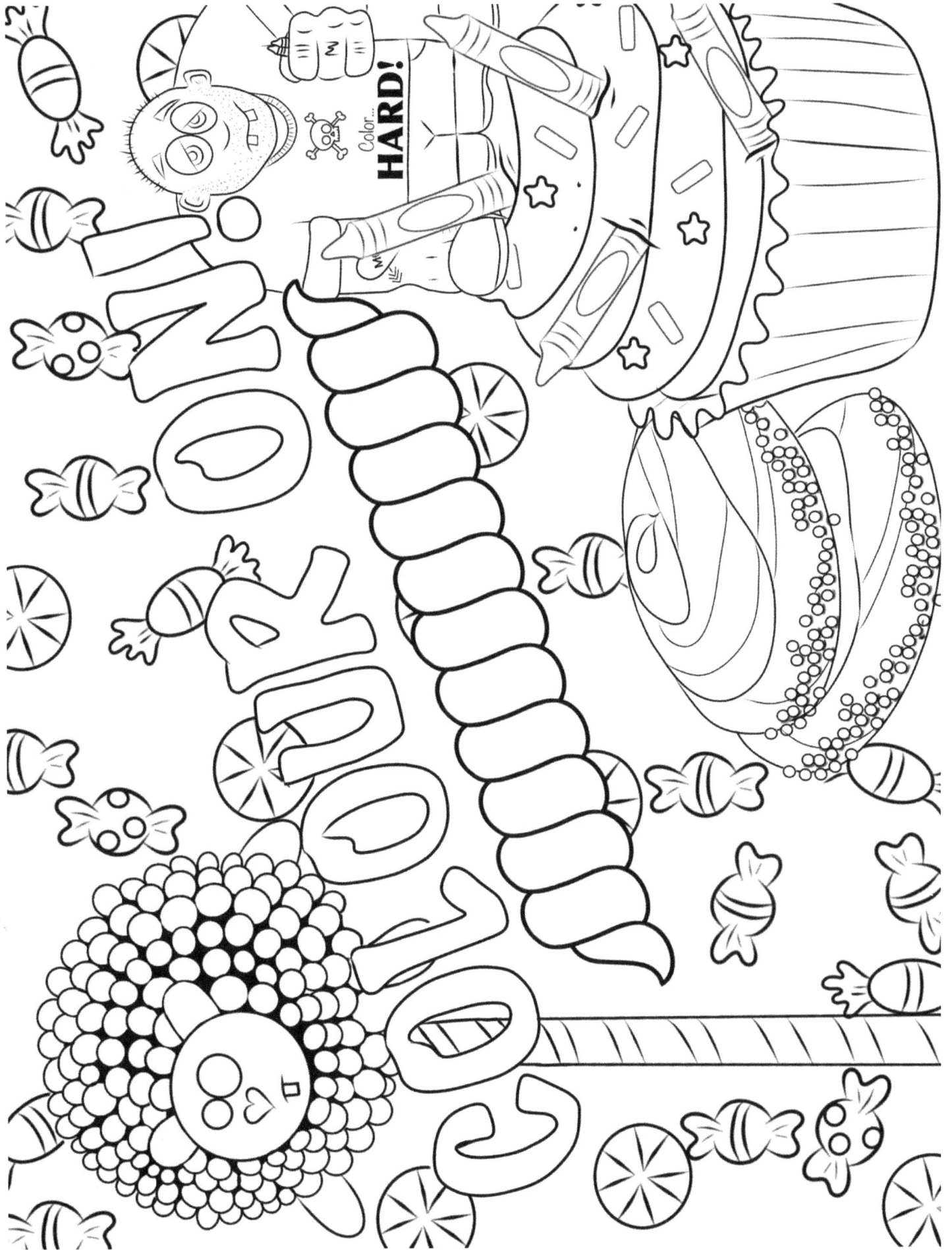

Color... **HARD!**

I'M NOT

A FOOD

COLORING

You can learn more about J.A. Early Riser & T.J. Crayons online.

- Full interview online: http://coloronmag.com/article/a-chat-with-absurdians-j-a-early-riser-and-t-j-crayons/
- Their website: http://maniacalconfessions.com
- Their Etsy shop: https://www.etsy.com/shop/ManiacalConfessions
- Join the Weirdos Facebook group: https://www.facebook.com/groups/ColoUringForWeirdos

Mary J. Winters-Meyer has been a creative since she was a child, but didn't consider herself an "artist" until she was in her 30s. Her first professional artistic adventure was in the world of bead weaving, where she had some success, winning several awards for her artwork, having an article published in *Bead & Button*, and self-publishing a bead pattern book. Her "real job" designing websites kept her from pursuing an artistic career at that time, keeping her busy for over 15 years.

In 2013, Mary started drawing her mandala-inspired artwork with science fiction and fantasy themes. That art eventually led to her foray into the coloring world, and in 2015 she began exploring that world full time. Her Facebook group, Coloring Books for Adults, has been tremendously successful, gaining over 30,000 members in less than a year. Members enjoy posting their colored works and sharing their passion for coloring in a positive atmosphere.

Additionally, Mary hosts a coloring review blog, also titled Coloring Books for Adults. The site features both written and video reviews of coloring books and products. Her reviews are also included in *Color On! Magazine*.

In October 2015, Mary launched *Color On! Magazine*. The magazine is now available both as a digital subscription and a full color printed issue, with both articles and coloring pages for colorists to enjoy. Print anthologies like this one are also published every three months, with the designs from the three magazine issues.

You can learn more about Mary online:
- Join Mary's Facebook group at https://www.facebook.com/groups/ColoringBooksForAdults
- Coloring Books for Adults review blog: http://AdultColoringBooks.com
- *Color On! Magazine*: http://ColorOnMag.com
- *Color On! Magazine* Facebook page: https://www.facebook.com/ColorOnMag
- *Color On! Magazine* Etsy shop: http://www.etsy.com/shop/ColorOnMagazine
- Mary's artwork for sale: http://tangitude.com
- Mary's books on Amazon: http://tinyurl.com/Tangitude

Mary J. Winters-Meyer has been a creative since she was a child, but didn't consider herself an "artist" until she was in her 30s. Her first professional artistic adventure was in the world of bead weaving, where she had some success, winning several awards for her artwork, having an article published in *Bead & Button*, and self-publishing a bead pattern book. Her "real job" designing websites kept her from pursuing an artistic career at that time, keeping her busy for over 15 years.

In 2013, Mary started drawing her mandala-inspired artwork with science fiction and fantasy themes. That art eventually led to her foray into the coloring world, and in 2015 she began exploring that world full time. Her Facebook group, Coloring Books for Adults, has been tremendously successful, gaining over 30,000 members in less than a year. Members enjoy posting their colored works and sharing their passion for coloring in a positive atmosphere.

Additionally, Mary hosts a coloring review blog, also titled Coloring Books for Adults. The site features both written and video reviews of coloring books and products. Her reviews are also included in *Color On! Magazine*.

In October 2015, Mary launched *Color On! Magazine*. The magazine is now available both as a digital subscription and a full color printed issue, with both articles and coloring pages for colorists to enjoy. Print anthologies like this one are also published every three months, with the designs from the three magazine issues.

You can learn more about Mary online:
- Join Mary's Facebook group at https://www.facebook.com/groups/ColoringBooksForAdults
- Coloring Books for Adults review blog: http://AdultColoringBooks.com
- *Color On! Magazine*: http://ColorOnMag.com
- *Color On! Magazine* Facebook page: https://www.facebook.com/ColorOnMag
- *Color On! Magazine* Etsy shop: http://www.etsy.com/shop/ColorOnMagazine
- Mary's artwork for sale: http://tangitude.com
- Mary's books on Amazon: http://tinyurl.com/Tangitude

color me

Mary J. Winters-Meyer has been a creative since she was a child, but didn't consider herself an "artist" until she was in her 30s. Her first professional artistic adventure was in the world of bead weaving, where she had some success, winning several awards for her artwork, having an article published in *Bead & Button*, and self-publishing a bead pattern book. Her "real job" designing websites kept her from pursuing an artistic career at that time, keeping her busy for over 15 years.

In 2013, Mary started drawing her mandala-inspired artwork with science fiction and fantasy themes. That art eventually led to her foray into the coloring world, and in 2015 she began exploring that world full time. Her Facebook group, Coloring Books for Adults, has been tremendously successful, gaining over 30,000 members in less than a year. Members enjoy posting their colored works and sharing their passion for coloring in a positive atmosphere.

Additionally, Mary hosts a coloring review blog, also titled Coloring Books for Adults. The site features both written and video reviews of coloring books and products. Her reviews are also included in *Color On! Magazine*.

In October 2015, Mary launched *Color On! Magazine*. The magazine is now available both as a digital subscription and a full color printed issue, with both articles and coloring pages for colorists to enjoy. Print anthologies like this one are also published every three months, with the designs from the three magazine issues.

You can learn more about Mary online:
- Join Mary's Facebook group at https://www.facebook.com/groups/ColoringBooksForAdults
- Coloring Books for Adults review blog: http://AdultColoringBooks.com
- *Color On! Magazine*: http://ColorOnMag.com
- *Color On! Magazine* Facebook page: https://www.facebook.com/ColorOnMag
- *Color On! Magazine* Etsy shop: http://www.etsy.com/shop/ColorOnMagazine
- Mary's artwork for sale: http://tangitude.com
- Mary's books on Amazon: http://tinyurl.com/Tangitude

Mary J. Winters-Meyer has been a creative since she was a child, but didn't consider herself an "artist" until she was in her 30s. Her first professional artistic adventure was in the world of bead weaving, where she had some success, winning several awards for her artwork, having an article published in *Bead & Button*, and self-publishing a bead pattern book. Her "real job" designing websites kept her from pursuing an artistic career at that time, keeping her busy for over 15 years.

In 2013, Mary started drawing her mandala-inspired artwork with science fiction and fantasy themes. That art eventually led to her foray into the coloring world, and in 2015 she began exploring that world full time. Her Facebook group, Coloring Books for Adults, has been tremendously successful, gaining over 30,000 members in less than a year. Members enjoy posting their colored works and sharing their passion for coloring in a positive atmosphere.

Additionally, Mary hosts a coloring review blog, also titled Coloring Books for Adults. The site features both written and video reviews of coloring books and products. Her reviews are also included in *Color On! Magazine*.

In October 2015, Mary launched *Color On! Magazine*. The magazine is now available both as a digital subscription and a full color printed issue, with both articles and coloring pages for colorists to enjoy. Print anthologies like this one are also published every three months, with the designs from the three magazine issues.

You can learn more about Mary online:
- Join Mary's Facebook group at https://www.facebook.com/groups/ColoringBooksForAdults
- Coloring Books for Adults review blog: http://AdultColoringBooks.com
- *Color On! Magazine*: http://ColorOnMag.com
- *Color On! Magazine* Facebook page: https://www.facebook.com/ColorOnMag
- *Color On! Magazine* Etsy shop: http://www.etsy.com/shop/ColorOnMagazine
- Mary's artwork for sale: http://tangitude.com
- Mary's books on Amazon: http://tinyurl.com/Tangitude

Introducing... Marshal Early Riser and the Gallumphing Grammar Gal!
Saving the West one crayon-crazed villain at a time.

You can learn more about J.A. Early Riser & T.J. Crayons online.

- Full interview online: http://coloronmag.com/article/a-chat-with-absurdians-j-a-early-riser-and-t-j-crayons/
- Their website: http://maniacalconfessions.com
- Their Etsy shop: https://www.etsy.com/shop/ManiacalConfessions
- Join the Weirdos Facebook group: https://www.facebook.com/groups/ColoUringForWeirdos

Mary J. Winters-Meyer has been a creative since she was a child, but didn't consider herself an "artist" until she was in her 30s. Her first professional artistic adventure was in the world of bead weaving, where she had some success, winning several awards for her artwork, having an article published in *Bead & Button*, and self-publishing a bead pattern book. Her "real job" designing websites kept her from pursuing an artistic career at that time, keeping her busy for over 15 years.

In 2013, Mary started drawing her mandala-inspired artwork with science fiction and fantasy themes. That art eventually led to her foray into the coloring world, and in 2015 she began exploring that world full time. Her Facebook group, Coloring Books for Adults, has been tremendously successful, gaining over 30,000 members in less than a year. Members enjoy posting their colored works and sharing their passion for coloring in a positive atmosphere.

Additionally, Mary hosts a coloring review blog, also titled Coloring Books for Adults. The site features both written and video reviews of coloring books and products. Her reviews are also included in *Color On! Magazine*.

In October 2015, Mary launched *Color On! Magazine*. The magazine is now available both as a digital subscription and a full color printed issue, with both articles and coloring pages for colorists to enjoy. Print anthologies like this one are also published every three months, with the designs from the three magazine issues.

You can learn more about Mary online:
- Join Mary's Facebook group at https://www.facebook.com/groups/ColoringBooksForAdults
- Coloring Books for Adults review blog: http://AdultColoringBooks.com
- *Color On! Magazine*: http://ColorOnMag.com
- *Color On! Magazine* Facebook page: https://www.facebook.com/ColorOnMag
- *Color On! Magazine* Etsy shop: http://www.etsy.com/shop/ColorOnMagazine
- Mary's artwork for sale: http://tangitude.com
- Mary's books on Amazon: http://tinyurl.com/Tangitude

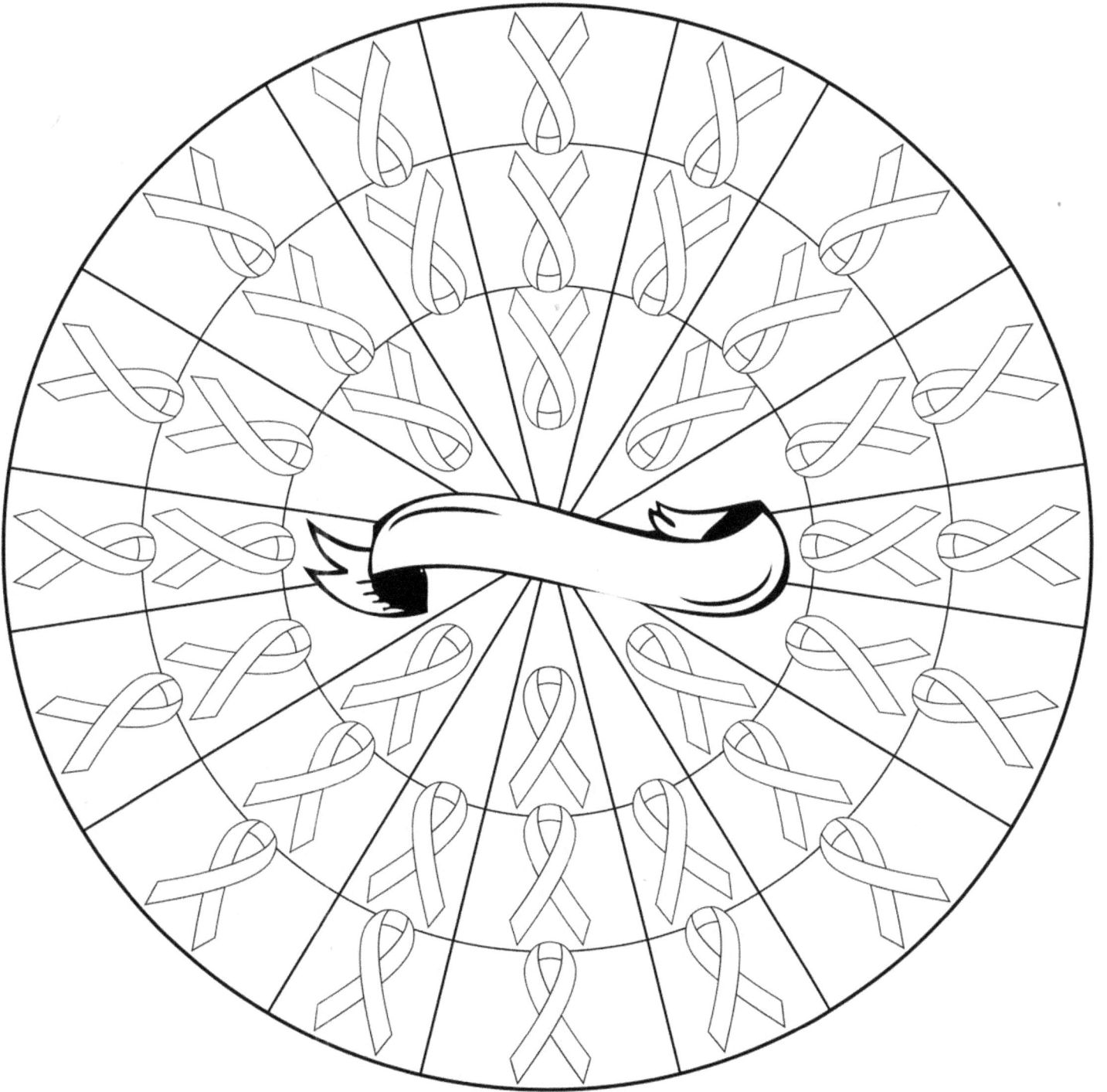

Mary J. Winters-Meyer has been a creative since she was a child, but didn't consider herself an "artist" until she was in her 30s. Her first professional artistic adventure was in the world of bead weaving, where she had some success, winning several awards for her artwork, having an article published in *Bead & Button*, and self-publishing a bead pattern book. Her "real job" designing websites kept her from pursuing an artistic career at that time, keeping her busy for over 15 years.

In 2013, Mary started drawing her mandala-inspired artwork with science fiction and fantasy themes. That art eventually led to her foray into the coloring world, and in 2015 she began exploring that world full time. Her Facebook group, Coloring Books for Adults, has been tremendously successful, gaining over 30,000 members in less than a year. Members enjoy posting their colored works and sharing their passion for coloring in a positive atmosphere.

Additionally, Mary hosts a coloring review blog, also titled Coloring Books for Adults. The site features both written and video reviews of coloring books and products. Her reviews are also included in *Color On! Magazine*.

In October 2015, Mary launched *Color On! Magazine*. The magazine is now available both as a digital subscription and a full color printed issue, with both articles and coloring pages for colorists to enjoy. Print anthologies like this one are also published every three months, with the designs from the three magazine issues.

You can learn more about Mary online:
- Join Mary's Facebook group at https://www.facebook.com/groups/ColoringBooksForAdults
- Coloring Books for Adults review blog: http://AdultColoringBooks.com
- *Color On! Magazine*: http://ColorOnMag.com
- *Color On! Magazine* Facebook page: https://www.facebook.com/ColorOnMag
- *Color On! Magazine* Etsy shop: http://www.etsy.com/shop/ColorOnMagazine
- Mary's artwork for sale: http://tangitude.com
- Mary's books on Amazon: http://tinyurl.com/Tangitude

Many of us color because it helps us deal with chronic illnesses or tragedies in our lives. That thought inspired this support ribbon mandala, which is also offered as a free download in my Facebook group Coloring Books for Adults, and on my blog at http://AdultColoringBooks.com. I always include it as one of the designs in my printed books.

Color the ribbons to match one or more support colors to fit your own struggles, or those of family and friends. If you're not sure if your particular condition has a ribbon color, you'd be amazed! Do an internet search and you'll probably find one! Or choose a color that represents your own inner thoughts and feelings. The center banner can be used to list the condition, or the name of the person you are supporting.

Test your colors

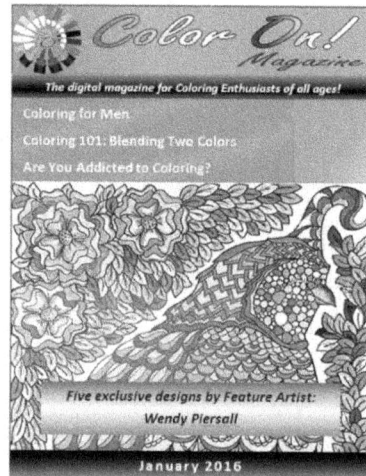

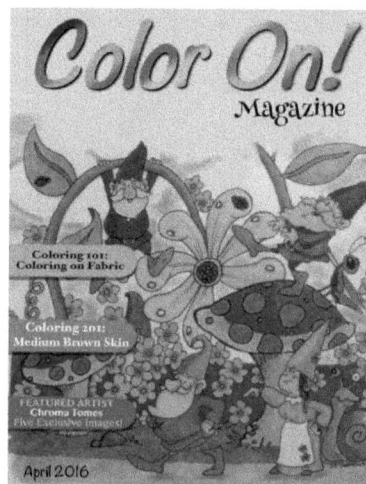

Test your colors

Coloring Books for Adults

A comprehensive review site for coloring enthusiasts of all ages

Trying to decide what coloring books you want?

Prefer to see the designs in the book before purchasing?

Need advice on what markers or pencils to use?

We can help!

www.AdultColoringBooks.com

Join Us on Facebook!

- Share your colored designs
- enjoy free coloring pages from artists
- learn new techniques
- participate in contests and giveaways

facebook.com/groups/ColoringBooksForAdults

Test your colors

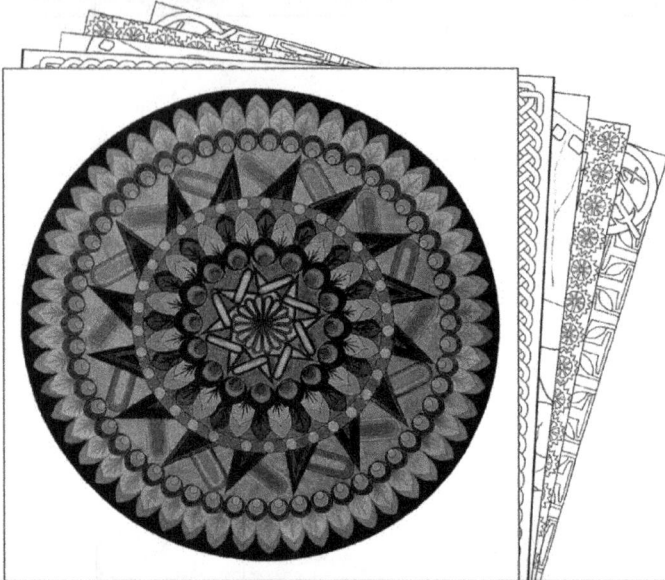

Test your colors

JOIN THE FUN!
in the....

ColoUring for
WEIRDOS

FACEBOOK Group!

EMBRACE YOUR INNER
WEIRDO

Bring on
The
WEIRDOS

- •WIN PRIZES
- •Try fun Weekly Weirdo challenges
- •Share your coloUred pictures!
- •Unite with your fellow Weirdos
- •HAVE A BLAST!
- •Browse other cool (and weird) coloring books
- •Find FREE coloUring pages!
- **JOIN TODAY!**

Test your colors

www.ingramcontent.com/pod-product-compliance
Lightning Source LLC
Chambersburg PA
CBHW080017280326
41934CB00015B/3381